John Calvin

Man of God's Word,
Written & Preached

By the same author

Both Sides Now:
Ecclesiastes and the Human Condition

Abortion:
Open Your Mouth for the Dumb

The Milk of the Word:
An Introduction to the Christian Faith

A Handful of Pebbles –
Theological Liberalism and the Church

John Calvin

Man of God's Word, *Written & Preached*

Peter Barnes

THE BANNER OF TRUTH TRUST

THE BANNER OF TRUTH TRUST

3 Murrayfield Road, Edinburgh EH12 6EL, UK
P.O. Box 621, Carlisle, PA 17013, USA

*

© Peter Barnes 2011

*

ISBN-13: 978 1 84871 121 1

*

Typeset in 11/15 Sabon Oldstyle Figures at
the Banner of Truth Trust, Edinburgh

Printed in the U.S.A. by
Versa Press, Inc.,
East Peoria, IL

Contents

Preface

Martin Luther commented that 'once the pure and certain Word is taken away, there remains no consolation, no salvation, no hope.' By and large, that is where the church found itself just before the Reformation, and by and large that is where the church finds itself today. B. B. Warfield claimed that Calvin's greatest contribution to theology was probably his teaching on the doctrine of the work of the Holy Spirit. True enough, but every doctrine is based on the Word of God. How God communicates to us, and how we make that known, have always been crucial issues, and continue to be so in our own corrupt and superstitious days.

No man did more in the Reformation period to point the church back to God's inerrant Word than John Calvin. Because of his faithfulness to Scripture, he was enabled to put forward a view of revelation which, we may be confident, reflects the mind of God himself. Having articulated Scripture's claims concerning itself, Calvin laboured, as few others have, to make this revelation known to his own hearers and, thankfully, to generations that succeeded him. The church owes a great debt to Calvin as a theologian, as a commentator, and as a preacher. Hopefully, this small book will indicate something of that debt, and, more importantly, help Christians to read and hear Scripture more cogently as God's true Word to helpless sinners.

PETER BARNES
Sydney
December 2010

1

John Calvin and God's Word, Written

'WHAT PASTURE IS TO THE BEAST, the nest for the birds, the stream for fish, the Scriptures are for believing souls.'[1] So wrote Martin Luther, in a sentence that indicates the centrality that the Bible was to have in the daily life of the church of the Reformation. Before the hostile Diet of Worms in April 1521, Luther stood alone with only the Scriptures to speak for him. Here he uttered those well-known words:

---

[1] Cited in P. Lehmann, 'The Reformers' Use of the Bible' in *Theology Today*, vol. 3, no. 3, 1946, p. 333.

Unless I am convinced by Scripture and plain reason—I do not accept the authority of popes and councils, for they have contradicted each other—my conscience is captive to the Word of God. I cannot and I will not recant anything, for to go against conscience is neither right nor safe. God help me. Amen.

He may have added, 'Here I stand, I can do no other, so help me, God.'[2]

The Sufficiency of Scripture

This firm belief in the sufficiency of God's inerrant Word was a direct challenge to the teachings of the medieval church, as exemplified, for example, in the writings of Duns Scotus. The influential 'Doctor Subtilis', as he was known, declared that 'Nothing is to be held as of the substance of the faith except that which can be expressly derived from Scripture or which is expressly declared by the church.'[3] Against this, the Reformers claimed that the Scriptures alone

[2] Cf. R. H. Bainton, *Here I Stand*, (New York: Abingdon, 1950), p. 185.

[3] Cited in B. A. Gerrish, 'Biblical Authority and the Continental Reformation' in *Scottish Journal of Theology*, vol. 10, no. 4, 1957, p. 339.

supplied the church's rule of faith and practice. Hence in the *Institutes*, the second generation Reformer of Geneva, John Calvin (1509-1564), stated that the power of the church is 'not infinite but subject to the Lord's Word and, as it were, enclosed within it'.[4] Calvin went on to point out the differences between the apostles and their successors:

> the former were sure and genuine scribes of the Holy Spirit, and their writings are therefore to be considered oracles of God; but the sole office of others is to teach what is provided and sealed in the Holy Scriptures.[5]

To Calvin, the divine authority of the church could only be located in the Word of God. The Bible provides the only reliable means whereby man can know God, and 'no one can get the slightest taste of right and sound doctrine unless he be a pupil of Scripture.'[6] In opposition both to the Roman Catholic emphasis on ecclesiastical tradition and to the enthusiasts' reliance on dreams and visions,

[4] Calvin, *Institutes of the Christian Religion*, IV, viii, 4.

[5] *Institutes*, IV, viii, 9.

[6] *Institutes*, IV, vi, 2.

Calvin asserted that 'daily oracles are not sent from heaven, for it pleased the Lord to hallow his truth to everlasting remembrance in the Scripture alone'.[7] Randall Zachman's conclusion regarding Calvin must therefore be rejected as paying insufficient attention to Scripture itself and to Calvin's commitment to its final and unrivalled authority:

> Oral tradition . . . not only lies behind Scripture, but it also accompanies it throughout its history, and teaches both Israel and the Christian community practices that cannot be found in Scripture.[8]

To Calvin, the troubles that beset Christendom in the sixteenth century were directly related to the papacy's refusal to accept Scripture as God's all-sufficient Word.

Calvin did maintain something like the traditional Thomist view that God can be known from nature and from Scripture. Nature, however, is not enough:

---

[7] *Institutes,* I, vii, 1.

[8] Randall Zachman, 'Oracles, Visions, and Oral Tradition: Calvin on the Foundation of Scripture' in *Interpretation,* vol. 63, no. 2, April 2009, p. 129.

if men were taught only by nature, they would hold
to nothing certain or solid or clear-cut, but would
be so tied to confused principles as to worship an
unknown god (cf. *Acts* 17:23).[9]

He referred to Plato as 'the most religious' and 'the
most circumspect' of the philosophers—but one who
still failed to know God in a saving way.[10] So far as
God was concerned, the insights of the philosophers
were like a lightning flash which vanished so swiftly
that the traveller was soon plunged into darkness
again.[11] Hence the need for God's Word:

> Scripture, gathering up the otherwise confused
> knowledge of God in our minds, having dispersed
> our dullness, clearly shows us the true God.[12]

All revelation of God outside of Scripture is uncertain. Scripture alone is the sufficient Word of God:

> let us remember to observe one rule of modesty
> and sobriety, which is, not to speak, or think, or
> even desire to know, concerning obscure subjects,

---

[9] *Institutes,* I, v, 12.

[10] *Institutes,* I, v, 11.

[11] *Institutes,* II, ii, 18.

[12] *Institutes,* I, vi, 1.

anything beyond the information given us in the divine Word.[13]

Like the Bible itself (e.g. *Deut.* 4:2; *Mark* 7:1-13), Calvin taught that 'everything pertaining to Christianity was prescribed and included in the Scriptures.'[14] As he put it in his sermons on Ephesians:

> It is God who must reign over us and have such mastery among us that we neither add anything to his pure Word, nor take anything from it.[15]

Scripture testifies to its own sufficient authority, and needs no *imprimatur* from the Church:

> Scripture exhibits fully as clear evidence of its own truth as white and black things do of their colour, or sweet and bitter things do of their taste.[16]

Modern Debates about the Authority of Scripture

While there can be no doubt about Calvin's position on the sufficiency of Scripture, there has been

[13] *Institutes,* I, xiv, 4.

[14] *Institutes,* IV, xix, 9.

[15] John Calvin, *Sermons on the Epistle to the Ephesians* (Edinburgh: Banner of Truth, 1562 in French, 1577 in English, revised 1975), p. 543.

[16] *Institutes,* I, vii, 2.

much debate about his teaching on the authority of the Word, especially concerning the question of the Bible's inerrancy. Stephen Holmes has declared this debate to be 'sterile', adding that Calvin can 'at times sound like both Warfield and Barth'.[17] Such a pronouncement underestimates the importance of what is at stake, and misinterprets Calvin's reverence for God's Word. T. H. L. Parker has reason to write that

> Calvin's concept of Scripture as the Word of God presents probably the most difficult problem in all his theology, one on which much has been written and about which there is considerable disagreement.[18]

On the one hand, R. E. Davies has concluded that 'Calvin committed himself to a completely verbal and mechanical theory of inspiration.'[19] By 'mechanical', Davies presumably means that, in the act of

[17] Stephen Holmes, 'Calvin on Scripture' in Neil B. MacDonald and Carl Trueman (eds), *Calvin, Barth, and Reformed Theology* (Eugene: Wipf and Stock, 2008), p.149, n2.

[18] T. H. L. Parker, *Calvin's New Testament Commentaries* (London: SCM, 1971), p. 56.

[19] R. E. Davies, *The Problem of Authority in the Continental Reformers* (London: Epworth, 1946), p. 114.

inspiration, the divine author—the Holy Spirit—completely obliterated all traces of the humanity of the human authors, namely the prophets and apostles. On the other hand, most modern scholars have opted for the other extreme of denying that Calvin ever taught the doctrine of the verbal inspiration of Holy Scripture. This latter interpretation has been put forward by J. T. McNeill,[20] François Wendel,[21] R. S. Wallace,[22] J. K. S. Reid,[23] Richard Prust,[24] I. S. Palmer,[25] and Wilhelm Niesel.[26] In 1918 at Safenwil, Karl Barth famously wrote:

> The historical-critical method of Biblical investigation has its rightful place: it is concerned with the

[20] J. T. McNeill, 'John Calvin: Doctor Ecclesiae' in J. H. Bratt (ed.), *The Heritage of John Calvin* (Michigan: Eerdmans, 1973), p. 13.

[21] F. Wendel, *Calvin* (London: Collins, 1974), pp. 159-160.

[22] R. S. Wallace, *Calvin's Doctrine of the Word and Sacrament* (Edinburgh: Oliver and Boyd, 1953), p. 114.

[23] J. K. S. Reid, *The Authority of Scripture* (London: Methuen and Co, 1957), p. 38.

[24] R. C. Prust, 'Was Calvin a Biblical Literalist?' in *Scottish Journal of Theology*, vol. 20, no. 3, 1967, p. 324.

[25] I. S. Palmer, 'The Authority and Doctrine of Scripture in the Thought of John Calvin' in *Evangelical Quarterly*, vol. 49, no. 1, 1977, p. 34.

[26] W. Niesel, *The Theology of Calvin* (London: Lutterworth, 1956), p. 31.

preparation of the intelligence—and this can never be superfluous. But, were I driven to choose between it and the venerable doctrine of Inspiration, I should without hesitation adopt the latter, which has a broader, deeper, more important justification. The doctrine of Inspiration is concerned with the labour of apprehending, without which no technical equipment, however complete is of any use whatever. Fortunately, I am not compelled to choose between the two.[27]

David Puckett is thus not alone in wanting to place Calvin in the same camp as Barth.[28]

Many of these scholars seem to have looked for evidence to bolster a pre-determined conclusion; and so the debate has come to resemble one of those inns in Spain to which one brings one's own food and drink. A far more satisfying conclusion is that of E. A. Dowey, a man who certainly does not adhere fully to Calvin's views. Dowey writes that 'There is no hint anywhere in Calvin's writings that the original text contained

[27] Karl Barth, *The Epistle to the Romans,* translated from the sixth edition by Edwyn C. Hoskyns (London: Oxford University Press, 1933), p. 1.

[28] David Puckett, *John Calvin's Exegesis of the Old Testament* (Louisville: Westminster John Knox Press, 1995), p. 144.

any flaws at all.'[29] Indeed, he adds: 'To Calvin the theologian, an error in Scripture is unthinkable.'[30] It will be seen that Calvin rejected any mechanical theory of inspiration, but he accepted what later became known as the complete verbal inspiration and inerrancy of Scripture.

The Humanity of Scripture

Calvin's writings contain no systematic analysis of the method of biblical inspiration, but a reasonably clear and coherent picture emerges from his commentaries and his magisterial work, the *Institutes of the Christian Religion*.

The first point that needs to be made is that Calvin was no proponent of the mechanical theory of inspiration; he fully accepted the humanity of the Scriptures. He noted, for example, the faults in the apostle Paul's literary style, but added that

the singular providence of God has passed on to us these profound mysteries in the garb of a poor style,

[29] E. A. Dowey, *The Knowledge of God in Calvin's Theology* (New York: Columbia University Press, 1952), p. 100.

[30] E. A. Dowey, *The Knowledge of God in Calvin's Theology*, p. 104.

so that our faith might not depend on the power of human eloquence, but on the efficacy of the Spirit alone.[31]

With regard to the unfinished sentence in Romans 8:12-13, Calvin had no hesitation in writing that 'Paul's sentence here is defective'.[32] Referring to the Epistle to the Hebrews, Calvin deduced that 'The manner of teaching and the style sufficiently show that Paul was not the author.'[33]

Calvin also noticed the differences in the language of First and Second Peter, and surmised that 2 Peter was not written by Peter himself, but 'one of his disciples composed by his command.'[34] A better explanation might be that Peter wrote his Second Epistle by himself, but that Silvanus helped to improve his style in the First Epistle (*1 Pet.* 5:12). Whatever the case, Calvin recognised differences in writing styles, and hence noted that David and Isaiah possessed a pleasing literary style, while Amos,

[31] Calvin, *Commentary,* Romans 5:15.

[32] Calvin, *Commentary,* Romans 8:12-13.

[33] Calvin, 'Argument' in *Commentary on Hebrews.*

[34] Calvin, 'Argument' in *Commentary on 2 Peter.*

Jeremiah and Zechariah possessed a harsher style.[35] He described Ezekiel as 'more verbose than Isaiah, and even than Jeremiah', and 'not . . . so restricted or so polished'[36]—perhaps rather like Martin Bucer compared to Calvin himself! The Holy Spirit did not move the prophets and apostles to write in a style reminiscent of the great Attic prose of Plato or Demosthenes, for the transmission of divine truth is not dependent upon the literary attainments of the biblical authors. From the awkward expression in Romans 2:8, Calvin drew the rather daring conclusion that 'It is from other writers that eloquence is to be learned: here spiritual wisdom is to be sought in an inadequate literary style which lacks polish and refinement.'[37]

To Calvin, it was clear that God's inspiration of his prophets and apostles did not obliterate their humanity. After Ezekiel received his vision and part of his commission, he was silent for seven days (*Ezek.* 3:16). Calvin explained that this was so because

[35] *Institutes,* I, viii, 2.

[36] Calvin, *Commentary,* Ezekiel 3:10-11.

[37] Calvin, *Commentary,* Romans 2:8.

he did not distinctly understand what he was to say, and where he ought to begin. Hence it appears, that God acts by degrees towards his servants, so that he claims them for his own, then he shows them generally what duties and labours they have to discharge, and at length he sends them forth to the performance of their work, and the execution of their office.[38]

The Lord did not usually work by instantaneously turning his servants into mechanical stenographers.

Regarding the Old Testament prophets, Calvin adopted what might be called a kind of supernatural commonsense approach as to how their writings came into existence. He stated:

We must bear in mind that the Prophets did not literally write what they delivered to the people, nor did they treat only once of those things which are now extant with us: but we have in their books collected summaries and heads of those matters which they were wont to address to the people. Hosea, no doubt, very often descanted on the exile and the restoration of the people, forasmuch as he dwelt much on all the things which we have hitherto noticed. Indeed, the slowness and dullness of the people were such,

[38] Calvin, *Commentary*, Ezekiel 3:16-17.

that the same things were repeated daily. But it was enough for the Prophets to make and to write down a brief summary of what they taught in their discourses.[39]

Biblical critics of the modern era could have spared themselves much anxiety and reduced the level of speculation had they followed this seemingly obvious point that the prophets—and apostles, and even the Saviour himself for that matter—spoke for longer than we have recorded in Scripture, and gave similar discourses a number of times.

It is true that Calvin held that God 'accommodated' himself to man, and that the Scriptures are fully human documents. God speaks to us simply and clearly as we are. As he put it in his sermons on Ephesians: 'For God has stooped in such a way that all of us from the greatest to the least may be taught in familiar fashion by his Word.'[40] Commenting on Psalm 49:4 he speaks of this idea in more detail:

> The truths of revelation are so high as to exceed our comprehension; but, at the same time, the Holy

[39] Calvin, *Commentary,* Hosea 4:1-2.

[40] Calvin, *Sermons on the Epistle to the Ephesians*, p. 542.

Spirit has accommodated them so far to our capacity, as to render all Scripture profitable for instruction. None can plead ignorance: for the deepest and most difficult doctrines are made plain to the most simple and unlettered of mankind.[41]

This concept of 'stooping' or 'accommodation' on God's part is a crucial one in Calvin's thought. God accommodates himself to fallen, fragile, and foolish human beings, so 'who even of slight intelligence does not understand that, as nurses commonly do with infants, God is wont in a measure to "lisp" in speaking to us?'[42]

In his commentary on John 3:12, Calvin explains this more fully, and writes vigorously:

But it shows an extraordinary degree of wickedness, that we yield less reverence to God speaking to us, because he condescends to our ignorance; and, therefore, when God prattles to us in Scripture in a rough and popular style, let us know that this is done on account of the love which he bears to us.[43]

---

[41] Calvin, *Commentary,* Psalm 49:4. See too Ford Lewis Battles, 'God Was Accommodating Himself to Human Capacity' in *Interpretation,* vol. 31, January 1977, pp. 19-38.

[42] Calvin, *Institutes,* I, xiii, 1.

[43] Calvin, *Commentary,* John 3:12.

Neither 'lisps' nor 'prattles' seems the ideal word to explain the concept, but the picture is clearly one of an adult indulging in baby talk in order to communicate to a youngster.

For example, Calvin acknowledged that Saturn is larger than the moon, despite the fact that Genesis 1:16 calls the moon 'the lesser light', second to the sun, 'the greater light'. However, Calvin went on to point out that to human sight it appears differently, and because Moses was ordained

> a teacher as well of the unlearned and rude as of the learned, he could not otherwise fulfil his office than by descending to this grosser method of instruction.[44]

Jack Rogers considers that Calvin was conceding that there was scientific error in the writings of Moses, and adds that Calvin himself was indifferent to it.[45] Stephen Holmes too asks: 'Is this an admission of error into Scripture? I think the only adequate

[44] Calvin, *Commentary*, Genesis 1:15-16.

[45] J. Rogers, *Biblical Authority* (Waco: Word, 1977), pp. 28-29. See Donald McKim (ed.), *Calvin and the Bible* (Cambridge: Cambridge University Press, 2006), especially pp. 5-6, 290.

response is to say that the question did not greatly interest Calvin.'[46]

These responses miss Calvin's point, for there is none of the dualism in Calvin's thought that one finds in many post-Kantian thinkers. Calvin would never have agreed with Auguste Sabatier, the French Protestant theologian, who declared concerning science and piety: 'There cannot be conflict between the two orders, because they move on different planes and never meet.'[47] Rather, Moses was concerned with things as they appear to the naked eye, while the astronomer is concerned with things as they appear through the telescope.

Calvin was not addicted to any form of wooden literalism, where the text did not warrant such. As a Christian, he naturally saw that heaven and hell are the two ends of man, but he viewed the tortures of hell—notably of fire and also of darkness—as 'figuratively expressed'.[48] To cite a similar example,

[46] Stephen Holmes, 'Calvin on Scripture', p.157.

[47] Cited in H. D. McDonald, *Theories of Revelation: An Historical Study 1860-1960* (London: George Allen and Unwin, 1963), p. 55.

[48] *Institutes*, III, xxv, 12.

Christ's ascension to the right hand of the Father is a question 'not of the disposition of his body, but of the majesty of his authority'.[49] With some straining of the text, Calvin maintained that when the Apostle John says of Christ: 'In him is no sin', he 'does not speak of Christ personally, but of his whole body',[50] meaning the church. And for better or for worse, Calvin adopted the view that it was 'very improbable' that Hosea actually married Gomer, on the grounds that God would not make his prophet so contemptible in the eyes of his people, Israel. Hosea 1-3 therefore refers to a vision in the prophet's mind.[51] To Calvin, 'true' usually meant 'literal', but not invariably so.

One might also examine Calvin's treatment of the New Testament citations of the Old Testament. Calvin stated: 'We indeed know that the Apostles in quoting Scripture often used a freer language than the original; for they counted it enough to quote what was suitable to their subject; hence they made no

[49] *Institutes*, II, xvi, 15.

[50] Calvin, *Commentary*, 1 John 2:6.

[51] Calvin, *Commentaries on the Twelve Minor Prophets*, translated by John Owen, vol. 1 on Hosea (Michigan: Baker, repr. 1979), pp. 43-46.

great account of words'.[52] Moreover, in explaining the doctrine of the Trinity, Calvin did not consider it necessary to confine oneself 'syllable by syllable' to scriptural words, so long as the biblical teaching was maintained.[53] Thus the word 'consubstantial', while it does not occur in Scripture, is nevertheless acceptable because the teaching that the Son is of one substance with the Father is a biblical doctrine (cf. *John* 10:30).[54] J. K. S. Reid explains, with some justification, that Calvin's emphasis and interest was placed, not on the record as such, but on the content of the record.[55] This is true enough, provided it is not given a Barthian twist, for Calvin regarded the record of Scripture as wholly reliable and authoritative. Calvin combined the highest respect for Scripture with a willingness to seek out the genius behind it. Hence he wrote concerning practices such as women covering their heads and men kneeling to pray: 'the established custom of the region, or humanity itself

---

[52] Calvin, *Commentary*, Romans 3:4.

[53] *Institutes*, I, xiii, 3.

[54] *Institutes*, IV, viii, 16.

[55] J. K. S. Reid, *The Authority of Scripture*, p. 43.

and the rule of modesty, dictate what is to be done or avoided in these matters'.[56]

Occasionally, it would be fair to accuse Calvin of being somewhat careless or even cavalier in dealing with a passage. The use of repetition in 1 John 2:14 provides one such example. Without any evidence, Calvin declared that

> These repetitions I deem superfluous; and it is probable that when unskilful readers falsely thought that he spoke twice of little children, they rashly introduced the other two clauses.[57]

The textual evidence indicates that there was no interpolation but it was John who was indulging in repetition for the sake of emphasis—and Calvin was too impatient to see the point. It must be said that this is highly unusual in the Reformer.

Calvin had a full appreciation of the humanity of the Scriptures, and had no desire to interpret in any mechanical sense. Karl Barth claims that the humanity of the biblical authors necessarily entails their

---

[56] *Institutes,* IV, x, 31.

[57] Calvin, *Commentary,* 1 John 2:14. Calvin also omits the second half of 1 John 2:23, with little warrant for doing so.

fallibility, and so he writes of the gospel authors: 'within certain limits and therefore relatively they are all vulnerable and therefore capable of error even in respect of religion and theology'.[58] The Roman Catholic scholar, Bruce Vawter, also asserts that 'A human literature containing no error would indeed be a contradiction in terms, since nothing is more human than to err.'[59] Behind the apparent humility of this statement lies the assumption that man's capacity for error is greater than God's power to govern his own creation. Taken to its logical extremes, Vawter's view would require the conclusion that Christ himself sinned, since he is truly human. No such notion, which owes more to Platonism than to Christianity, appears in Calvin's writings—nor, for that matter, in the Bible.

The Fallibility of the Preacher

Calvin was not one who identified the inerrancy of Scripture with the infallibility of the preacher.

---

[58] Cf. K. Runia, *Karl Barth's Doctrine of Holy Scripture* (Michigan: Eerdmans, 1962), p. 60.

[59] B. Vawter, *Biblical Inspiration* (London: Hutchinson, 1972), p. 169.

He was most firm in all that he believed that Scripture clearly taught, but he was also aware that fallen human beings — even regenerate fallen human beings — would never grasp the full message of Scripture in this life. While liberal Biblical critics have referred complacently to the 'assured results' of Biblical Criticism, Calvin made no such claims for the evangelical preacher. In discussing whether 'forgive' and 'cleanse' in 1 John 1:9 should be regarded as synonyms, Calvin argued that they were not, but then added: 'If yet any one prefers another explanation, that he says the same thing twice over, I shall not object.'[60] On Hosea 1:11, where the day of Jezreel is said to be great, Calvin offered two possible explanations, namely that God would sow whom he had previously scattered, or as the calamity was grievous, so the return would be great. His conclusion was mild enough: 'This seems to be really the meaning of the Prophet.'[61] Such an approach is not uncommon in Calvin's writings, and indicates a mind that was clear of an assertive dogmatic spirit.

[60] Calvin, *Commentary,* 1 John 1:9.
[61] Calvin, Commentary, Hosea 1:11.

Even when Calvin was more decided, he could not be accused of being overbearing. There has been a long-standing debate as to whether the Greek word, ὅτι, in 1 John 2:12-14 should be translated as 'because' or 'that'. Calvin commented: 'The particle ὅτι is explained in two ways, but the meaning I have given to it is the best (sic), and agrees better with the context.'[62] In 1 John 4:19 Calvin discussed whether 'we love' should be regarded as indicative or imperative. He favoured the former, that John was simply saying that we love God rather than telling us to love him. Yet he adds:

> If, however, the imperative mood be preferred, the meaning would be nearly the same, that as God has freely loved us, we also ought now to love him.[63]

We do not find in Calvin any well-developed theory of Textual or Lower Criticism, but he was not unaware that the authority of Scripture did not rest on any particular textual transmission. For example, on the well-known Johannine Comma—the heavenly witness of the Father, the Word, and the Holy Spirit

---

[62] Calvin, *Commentary*, 1 John 2:13.

[63] Calvin, *Commentary*, 1 John 4:19.

in 1 John 5:7—Calvin tended to favour its inclusion. However, he was hardly dogmatic on the issue: 'But as even the Greek copies do not agree, I dare not assert any thing on the subject.'[64] Responding to those who pointed out that Cornelius was accepted by God before he was called to faith (*Acts* 10:2), whereas 1 John 5:12 says that 'he who does not have the Son of God does not have life', Calvin was content to issue the warning:

> But as God acts in ways hidden and wonderful, let us disregard those speculations which profit nothing, and hold only to that plain way of salvation, which he has made known to us.[65]

Calvin sought to stay within the boundaries that God has given human beings. When the murderous Duke of Guise was assassinated in 1563, some Huguenot zealots declared him to be anathema. Calvin had long prayed either for the Duke's conversion or his removal. Not far from death himself, Calvin sought to correct the zealots:

> To pronounce that he is damned, however, is to go

---

[64] Calvin, *Commentary*, 1 John 5:7.
[65] Calvin, *Commentary*, 1 John 5:12. See too on 1 John 5:17.

too far, unless one had some certain and infallible
mark of his reprobation. In which we must guard
against presumption and temerity, for there is none
can know that but the Judge before whose tribunal
we have all to render an account.[66]

In his 168th sermon on Deuteronomy, in explaining
Deuteronomy 29:19, he spoke of our need to pursue
all that God had revealed. Yet he also warned:

We may not . . . do as many fantastical heads do,
who covet to know this and that, whereof we have no
revelation in Holy Scripture . . . For it is the greatest
wisdom that can be in men, not to be inquisitive of
further things than God has revealed unto them, and
simply to content themselves with that which they
are able to conceive.[67]

The Full Authority of Scripture

Calvin held to the full humanity and the full divin-
ity of Holy Scripture. In a sermon on Deuteronomy,
he preached:

[66] Calvin, 'Letter to the Duchess of Ferrara', 24 January 1564, in
Tracts and Letters, vol. 7, ed. Jules Bonnet, tr. by Marcus Gilchrist
(Edinburgh: Banner of Truth, repr. 2009), p. 354.

[67] Calvin, *Sermons on Deuteronomy* (Edinburgh: Banner of Truth,
repr. 1987), p. 1044 (language modernized).

What is Holy Scripture but a declaration of the will of God? And so all that is there contained is as if God opened his sacred mouth to declare to us what he demands.[68]

Commenting on the classic text, 2 Timothy 3:16, Calvin was even more explicit:

This is the principle which distinguishes our religion from all others, that we know that God has spoken to us, and are fully convinced that the prophets did not speak at their own suggestion, but that, being organs of the Holy Spirit, they only uttered what they had been commissioned from heaven to declare. Whoever then wishes to profit in the Scriptures, let him, first of all, lay down this as a settled point, that the Law and the Prophets are not a doctrine delivered according to the will and pleasure of men, but dictated by the Holy Spirit.[69]

Alister McGrath has managed to be both true and misleading in his assertion that

Calvin does not believe that it is possible to reduce God or Christian experience to words. Christianity is not a verbal religion, but is experiential; it centres

---

[68] Cited in J. K. S. Reid, *The Authority of Scripture,* p. 34.

[69] Calvin, *Commentary,* 2 Timothy 3:16.

upon a transformative encounter of the believer with the risen Christ.[70]

Salvation is through Christ alone—the Bible is not our saviour—but Calvin did not shrink from asserting that

> we owe to the Scripture the same reverence which we owe to God; because it has proceeded from him alone, and has nothing belonging to man mixed with it.[71]

Calvin did not mean this in the docetic sense that the Scriptures were not human documents, but in the orthodox sense that they contain no human errors. Moses, for example,

> wrote his five books not only under the guidance of the Spirit of God, but as God himself had suggested them speaking out of his own mouth.[72]

In a similar way, God

> so dictated to the Four Evangelists what they should write that, while each had his own part, the whole

[70] Alister E. McGrath, *A Life of John Calvin* (Oxford: Basil Blackwell, 1990), p. 132.

[71] Calvin, *Commentary*, 2 Timothy 3:16.

[72] Calvin, *Commentary*, Exodus 31:18.

formed one complete body. It is for us now to blend the four in a mutual connexion, that we may let ourselves be taught as by the one mouth.[73]

In order to describe the method of inspiration, Calvin would often make use of the dreaded word 'dictated'. Commenting on Jeremiah 36:4-6, where the prophet repeats his message to Baruch, Calvin stated: 'the greater part of so many words must have escaped the Prophet, had not God dictated them again to him.'[74] Scripture is thus the work of God, and, as such, it cannot contain contradictions, for, as Calvin said: 'He [the Holy Spirit] is the author of the Scriptures: he cannot be mutable and inconsistent with himself.'[75] Whereas Karl Barth regarded the Apostles James and Paul as contradictory, and even Luther was caused much anguish by this old problem, Calvin explained simply that

> If you would make James agree with the rest of Scripture and with himself, you must understand the word *justify* in another sense than Paul takes it.[76]

[73] Calvin, *Commentary,* 'Argument' of John's Gospel.

[74] Calvin, *Commentary,* Jeremiah 36:4-6.

[75] Cited in H. J. Forstman, *Word and Spirit* (California: Stanford University Press, 1962), p. 59.

[76] *Institutes,* III, xvii, 12.

Calvin's deep reverence for Scripture can be seen in his treatment of two awkward examples of apparent errors in Scripture. In Genesis 46:27 it is said that seventy souls went down into Egypt, whereas Acts 7:14 puts the number at seventy-five. Calvin attributed this to 'an error of the transcribers', not of the original authors, although he added that since the Septuagint (the Greek version of the Old Testament, translated in the third or second century B.C.) refers to 75 souls, a second explanation was possible. His mild conclusion was:

> If any one, however, chooses rather to suppose that Luke in this instance accommodated himself to the rude and illiterate, who were accustomed to the Greek version, I do not contend with them.[77]

This second explanation is regarded by John Murray as somewhat ill-advised.[78] Yet Calvin's whole exegesis indicates his deep reluctance to attribute any error to Scripture.

A similar problem confronts the reader in Matthew 27:9 where an apparent paraphrase from Zechariah

[77] Calvin, *Commentary*, Genesis 46:8.

[78] John Murray, *Calvin on Scripture and Divine Sovereignty* (Welwyn: Evangelical Press, 1979), p. 31.

is attributed to Jeremiah. With uncharacteristic haste, Calvin declared, 'obviously Jeremiah's name is put in error for Zechariah. Nothing of this sort is said of Jeremiah, or anything like it.'[79] In fact, Jeremiah 18:2; 19:2, 11 and 32:6-9 may also stand at the back of this quotation, and Matthew may have only named the major prophet, in the same way that Mark 1:2-3 is attributed to Isaiah when it is clear that both Isaiah and Malachi are quoted. Whatever the case, Calvin's comment is mild enough: 'How the name of Jeremiah crept in I cannot confess to know nor do I make much of it.'[80] Luther was rather more reckless in his views, and swept aside all difficulties, claiming that 'Those people who labour over non-essential matters of this sort are more than mad.'[81] Actually, more is at stake than Luther in his more agitated moments realised, and Calvin's more circumspect attitude, while itself not always well-founded, has much to commend it. It was with good reason that

[79] Calvin, *Commentary,* Matthew 27:9.

[80] Calvin, *Commentary,* Matthew 27:9.

[81] Martin Luther, *Lectures on the Minor Prophets,* III, in *Works,* vol. 20, ed. by H. C. Oswald (St Louis: Concordia, 1973), p. 125.

Calvin opposed Sebastian Castellio, the Rector of the College at Geneva, when the latter denied the canonicity of the Song of Songs.

Word and Spirit

Calvin's view of Scripture is thus somewhat parallel to his view of Christ—just as Christ is both God and man, so is Scripture both divine and human. Yet, although Calvin regarded the Bible as doctrinally sufficient in itself and as the only full revelation of the mind of God, he still maintained that the external Word was not enough for salvation. The Reformer declared that 'without the illumination of the Holy Spirit, the Word can do nothing.'[82] As H. J. Forstman has pointed out, Calvin's theology has a dual cast, resting on Word and Spirit.[83] In the *Institutes*, Calvin summarised his view:

> God works in his elect in two ways: within, through his Spirit; without, through his Word. By his Spirit, illuminating their minds and forming their hearts to the love and cultivation of righteousness, he makes

[82] *Institutes*, III, ii, 33.
[83] H. J. Forstman, *Word and Spirit, passim*, especially p. 138.

them a new creation. By his Word, he arouses them to desire, to seek after, and to attain that same renewal.[84]

Wild-eyed visionaries and dry scholastics were alike repudiated by Calvin:

> It is no less unreasonable to boast of the Spirit without the Word, than it would be an absurd thing to bring forward the Word itself without the Spirit.[85]

Calvin's distinction between the work of the Word and that of the Spirit has prompted J. K. S. Reid to conclude: 'If this separation be recognized, it is impossible to impose upon Calvin a doctrine of verbal infallibility and inerrancy.'[86] However, Reid often adopts the role of a Barthian Don Quixote, jousting with orthodox windmills. The fact that Calvin distinguished between Word and Spirit does not mean that he thought the Word was capable of error. Rather, he meant that without the Spirit, the Word could not be understood by sinful human beings. Noting Isaiah 55:11, Calvin

[84] *Institutes,* II, v, 5.

[85] Cited in R. S. Wallace, *Calvin's Doctrine of the Word and Sacrament,* pp. 98-99.

[86] J. K. S. Reid, *The Authority of Scripture,* p. 47.

commented: 'As the Word is efficacious for the salvation of believers, so it is abundantly efficacious for the condemning of the wicked.'[87]

The Centrality of Christ

One other aspect of Calvin's view of Scripture that needs to be pointed out is the centrality given to Christ. Noting Paul's words in Romans 1:3-4, Calvin declared that 'the whole Gospel is contained in Christ'.[88] In his commentary on John 5:39, Calvin made a similar point:

> First, then, we must hold that Christ cannot be properly known from anywhere but the Scriptures. And if that is so, it follows that the Scriptures should be read with the aim of finding Christ in them.[89]

The Old and New Testaments alike testify of Christ, for 'God never revealed himself without Christ.'[90] In keeping with the biblical revelation, Calvin explained that the prophecies of the Old Testament were dictated

[87] Calvin, *Commentary*, Isaiah 55:11.

[88] Calvin, *Commentary*, Romans 1:3.

[89] Calvin, *Commentary*, John 5:39.

[90] Calvin, *Commentary*, John 5:23.

by Christ.[91] From all this, Wilhelm Niesel[92] and J. K.
S. Reid[93] deduce the strange conclusion that Calvin's
emphasis on the centrality and finality of Christ as the
incarnate Word necessarily implies that the Bible cannot be identified with the Word of God. To quote Karl
Barth: 'we do the Bible poor and unwelcome honour
if we equate it . . . with revelation itself.'[94]

Calvin saw no such problem. On the contrary, the
infallible written Word is to lead us to the sinless
Word made flesh, and the Word made flesh is to lead
us back to the authoritative written Word. As R. C.
Sproul observes: 'The church cannot submit to the
authority of Christ without at the same time submit-
ting to the authority of the Scripture.'[95]

Nor is William Temple's conclusion any more
compelling than that of Niesel and Reid. Temple
claimed that where reliance upon infallibility comes

[91] Calvin, *Commentary,* 1 Peter 1:10-11.

[92] W. Niesel, *The Theology of Calvin,* pp. 31-33.

[93] J. K. S. Reid, *The Authority of Scripture,* p. 38.

[94] K. Barth, *Church Dogmatics,* I,1, ed. by G. Bromiley (Edinburgh:
T. & T. Clark), p. 112.

[95] R. C. Sproul, 'The Case for Inerrancy' in J. W. Montgomery (ed.),
God's Inerrant Word (Minnesota: Bethany, 1974), p. 259.

in, spirituality goes out.[96] It would be a formidable task indeed to defend the proposition that spirituality has been the preserve of liberal modernists. Calvin's own religion was warm and Christ-centred. Humbly he acknowledged that 'faith looks at nothing but the mercy of God and Christ dead and risen.'[97] Calvin well knew the limitations of the human intellect, and so he asked: 'How can the mind by its own leading come to search out God's essence when it cannot even get to its own?'[98] Man's unaided reason could never lead him to the triune God; hence God had to reveal himself in his Word. This means that, in Calvin's words, 'all who forsake the Word fall into idolatry.'[99] In an age when the radical obscurantism of so much of modern theology is treated as if it were inerrant and infallible — or even sensible in some cases — Calvin's words have proved prophetic: 'once we hold God's Word in contempt, we shake off all reverence for him.'[100]

---

[96] W. Temple, *Nature, Man and God* (London: MacMillan and Co., 1960), p. 353.

[97] Calvin, *Commentary*, Galatians 3:6.

[97] *Institutes*, I, xiii, 21.

[99] Calvin, *Commentary*, John 4:22.

[100] *Institutes*, II, i, 4.

Conclusion

In summary, Calvin's doctrine of Scripture, albeit with a few examples of untidiness, is generally distilled by both clarity and godliness. It possesses many aspects—the Bible is sufficient for what the church teaches, but the Holy Spirit is needed for that teaching to become efficacious; the Bible is a fully human document, but it is also God's inerrant Word; and more than all this, it points us to the Son of God, who for us sinful human beings, and for our salvation, came down from heaven. One could do no better than to close with Calvin's own words:

> Our wisdom ought to be nothing else than to embrace with humble teachableness, and at least without finding fault, whatever is taught in sacred Scripture.[101]

---

[101] *Institutes*, I, xviii, 4.

2

John Calvin and God's Word, Preached

JOHN CALVIN IS BETTER KNOWN as a commentator and theologian than a preacher, but he deserves his due as one who regularly proclaimed God's Word to God's people. As a rhetorician, he owed something to Cicero and Quintilian. In the first century A.D., Quintilian followed the style of Cicero in abandoning any emphasis on what was flashy and ornate, and replacing it with what was simple, concise and practical. He organized the practice of oratory into five canons: *inventio* (discovery of arguments), *dispositio* (arrangement of arguments), *elocutio* (expression or style), *memoria* (memorization), and *pronuntiatio* (delivery). Calvin's approach was not dissimilar, although he betrays no discernible anxiety to copy either Quintilian or Cicero.[1] Bruce Gordon has recently repeated the claim that Calvin re-read Cicero every year[2]—a claim which, while containing truth, is unlikely to be wholly true. In any case, in Bernard Cottret's simple and laconic estimation: 'Calvin was a man who spoke.'[3]

In 1535—the year before both Calvin's arrival in Geneva and the publication of the first edition of his *Institutes of the Christian Religion*—there were 245 Catholic clergy in Geneva, but these were replaced by 20 Protestant clerics.[4] Those were difficult days. By 1542 there were five preachers, including Calvin, in the city, but of the other four, the best educated had the worst style.[5] Wilhelmus H. Th. Moehn says

[1] Cf. Quirinus Breen, 'John Calvin and the Rhetorical Tradition' in *Church History*, vol. 26, March 1957, pp.3-21, especially p. 6.

[2] Bruce Gordon, *Calvin* (New Haven and London: Yale University Press, 2009), p. 4.

[3] Bernard Cottret, *Calvin: A Biography,* translated by M. Wallace McDonald (Michigan: Eerdmans, 2000), p. 288.

[4] Cited in Marvin Anderson, 'John Calvin: Biblical Preacher (1539-1564)' in *Scottish Journal of Theology,* vol. 42, no. 2, 1989, p. 168. Anderson does not give a time frame for the 20 Protestant clerics.

[5] T. H. L. Parker, *Calvin's Preaching* (Louisville: Westminster/ John

that by 1550 Calvin had seven preaching colleagues within Geneva itself, and ten in the congregations outside the city.[6] There were three city churches — St Pierre's (the former cathedral, and the place where Calvin ministered), St Gervais, and St Magdalene, with a catechism class for little children at noon each Sunday. In 1541, on Mondays, Tuesdays, and Fridays sermons were preached in the church of St Pierre one hour before the sermon in the other churches.[7] On Friday mornings a meeting of the *Congrégation* also took place. This was a kind of ministerial Bible study at which up to twenty ministers were present along with perhaps as many as forty lay people.[8]

From 1549 Calvin preached every weekday on alternate weeks, delivering more than 2,000 sermons on the Old Testament alone. (He spent a year, 1554-

---

Knox Press, 1992), p. 60.

[6] Wilhelmus H. Th. Moehn, *God Calls Us to His Service: The Relation Between God and His Audience in Calvin's Sermons on Acts* (ET, Geneva, 2001), p. 236.

[7] Draft Ecclesiastical Ordinances, September and October 1541 in J. K. S. Reid (ed), *Calvin: Theological Treatises* (Philadelphia: Westminster Press, Library of Christian Classics, 1954), p. 62.

[8] See Erik A. de Boer, 'The Presence and Participation of Laypeople in the Congrégations of the Company of Pastors in Geneva, in *Sixteenth Century Journal,* vol. XXXV, no.3, 2004, pp. 651-670.

5, on the book of Job and three years on Isaiah.)[9] All in all, Calvin preached an extraordinary number of sermons on the longer books of the Bible—notably, 200 on Deuteronomy, 174 on Ezekiel, and 189 on Acts.[10] Clearly, he had little time for preparation. His congregations sometimes included distinguished hearers, as during his series on Ephesians in 1558-59 when the Scottish Reformer, John Knox, was present.

While it seems that four stenographers were used to write down Calvin's biblical lectures,[11] the preservation of his sermons came about largely through the work of one remarkable stenographer, a French refugee named Denis Raguenier. He wrote down most of the Reformer's sermons, as they were being delivered, from about 1549 until his own death, which occurred in the winter of 1560-1. After each

[9] Marvin Anderson, p. 173.

[10] Dawn DeVries, 'Calvin's Preaching', in Donald K. McKim, *The Cambridge Companion to John Calvin* (Cambridge: Cambridge University Press, 2004), p. 111. Parker says that Raguenier's mathematics are slightly astray, and finds 175 sermons on Ezekiel and 201 on Deuteronomy (*Calvin's Preaching,* p. 157).

[11] John Crispin, 'To Christian readers, health' in Calvin, *Commentaries on the Twelve Minor Prophets,* tr. by John Owen, vol 1, Hosea (Michigan: Baker, reprinted 1979), pp. xxx-xxxi.

sermon, a bound copy was delivered to the deacons for safekeeping. However, over time these volumes came to lose some of their initial worth in the eyes of his fellow countrymen. In 1805 or 1806 a librarian in the Genevan library sold 2,000 unpublished sermons as scrap paper! Apparently, he found them hard to read, and perhaps he thought that the shelf-space they occupied in the library could be put to better use.[12] Hence many of Calvin's sermons on the Old Testament prophets have been lost to posterity, as well as many on the Gospels, the Acts, and the Epistles. With the recovery of three volumes of sermons on Isaiah by Max Engammare in the French Protestant Church in London's Soho Square, in 1995, it is estimated that about 1,500 of the Reformer's sermons have survived.[13]

[12] Marvin Anderson, p. 174. For more details, see John Calvin, *Sermons from Job,* selected and tr. by Leroy Nixon (Michigan: Baker, 1952, repr. 1979), p. x.

[13] Geoffrey Thomas, 'The Wonderful Discovery of John Calvin's Sermons' in *The Banner of Truth,* Issue 436, January 2000, p. 23; also Bernard Cottret, *Calvin: A Biography,* tr. M. Wallace McDonald (Michigan: Eerdmans, 2000), p. 289. For more details, see Wulfert de Greef, *The Writings of John Calvin,* Expanded Ed., tr. by Lyle D. Bierma (Louisville: Westminster John Knox Press, 2008), pp. 93-100.

It needs to be remembered that Calvin was never keen for his sermons to be published, partly because he regarded them as too localised in application to be of much benefit to a wider audience. As he put it:

> If I can hardly succeed in being slightly useful to the Church by compositions well worked over, how foolish I should be to claim a place for my spoken words among my published works.[14]

His editor, Conrad Badius commented in 1558 that '[Calvin] would rather have his sermons heard no farther than his own sheepfold.'[15] It appears that Calvin only came to consent to their publication because the profits derived thereby were used to support French refugees.[16] The exception to this rule concerns the so-called *Four Sermons*—on Psalm 16:4; Hebrews 13:13; Psalm 27:4, and 27:8—which were preached in 1549 and then revised and published with an

---

[14] Cited in Pete Wilcox, 'Calvin as commentator on the Prophets' in Donald McKim (ed.), *Calvin and the Bible* (Cambridge: Cambridge University Press, 2006), p. 117.

[15] Bernard Cottret, *Calvin: A Biography*, p. 292.

[16] See Wilhelmus H. Th. Moehn, *God Calls Us to His Service: The Relation Between God and His Audience in Calvin's Sermons on Acts* (ET, Geneva, 2001, pp. 191-192); also Herman J. Selderhuis, *John Calvin: A Pilgrim's Life,* translated by Albert Gootjes (Downers Grove: IVP, 2009), p. 131.

exposition on Psalm 87 in 1552. They all deal with the recurring problem of the Reformed Christian's obligation to worship in a godly way despite the hostility of Roman Catholic authorities.[17]

Calvin as Preacher

Calvin interpreted Ephesians 4:11 to mean that pastors and teachers belonged to two distinct offices. Hence a teacher might write commentaries while a pastor would preach sermons.[18] Calvin's sermons, therefore, dispense with the critical apparatus that can be found in his commentaries. His preaching and writing styles are similar in clarity, passion, and seriousness, but they differ in the use of repetition found in the sermons. Calvin preached extemporaneously, and seems to have carried only his Hebrew or Greek Testaments with him into the pulpit. Parker says that 'it is hard to see how one can escape the conclusion that Calvin used a Hebrew Bible when preaching on Isaiah.'[19] Presumably this was true of all

[17] See John Calvin, *Faith Unfeigned,* translated by Robert White (Edinburgh: Banner of Truth, 2010).
[18] John Calvin, *Sermons on Ephesians,* p. 365.
[19] Parker, *Calvin's Preaching,* p. 173.

his sermons on the Old Testament, and may be said, with less certainty, of his use of Greek in his sermons on the New Testament. Since Calvin cited texts from memory or used his own paraphrase, no two citations of the same text were necessarily identical.

Calvin made a virtue of this practice of carrying no written manuscript with him into the pulpit. In his well-known letter of 1548 written to the Protector Somerset (the regent of England at that time as Edward VI was only eleven years of age), Calvin noted that 'there is very little preaching of a lively kind in the kingdom, but . . . the greater part deliver it by way of reading from a written discourse.'[20] No doubt Calvin's very heavy workload put tremendous pressures on his time for sermon preparation, but his preference seems to have been not to rely upon a written manuscript, and certainly not to simply read from one in the pulpit. As he said of his sermons on Psalm 119, preached in 1553:

> I did not write [them] in my room, but they were printed exactly as someone had been able to collect

[20] Calvin, *Tracts and Letters,* vol. 5, p. 190.

them from my mouth in the church. There you see our style in the ordinary way of teaching.[21]

This is not to say that he did not try to prepare well. While preaching on the subject of not tempting God, from Deuteronomy 6:15-19, he said:

> It is all one as if I should step up into the pulpit, without vouchsafing to look upon any book, and fondly imagine to say thus in myself: truth, when I come thither, God will give me enough whereof to speak, and in the meanwhile I hold scorn to read, or to study beforehand what I shall speak, and come hither without minding how to apply the Holy Scripture to the edification of the people, by reason whereof I should play the presumptuous fool, and God also would put me to shame for my overboldness.[22]

In Calvin's estimation, trust is not the same as presumption.

Having said that, Calvin lived life on the run, as it were. In a letter to William Farel on 8 June 1554, he laments: 'I do not have the leisure to write now, as the hour for [my] lecture is at hand, and it has not yet been possible for me to consider carefully what I

---

[21] Cited in Bernard Cottret, *Calvin: A Biography*, p. 290.
[22] John Calvin, *Sermons on Deuteronomy*, p. 292.

am to say.'[23] Nevertheless, he continued on with his letter, and presumably went on to give his lecture rather under-prepared.

In 1932 George Johnson wrote:

> The entire service occupied about one hour, and since it included prayer and psalm, the sermon must have been delivered with great rapidity of utterance in order to keep within the time.[24]

Robert Godfrey too writes of Calvin, 'His sermons were usually about thirty minutes long.'[25] This must be regarded as unlikely in the extreme. Calvin suffered from asthma, and in any case, his sermons indicate a fair amount of interaction with the congregation, which would be impossible if he were racing through the sermon. The published sermons that we possess would be difficult to preach in much less than an hour. It is thus likely that he preached for about fifty minutes to an hour. T. H. L. Parker and Steven Lawson opt for about an hour,[26] while

[23] Calvin, Letter 1962, kindly tr. by Rev. Dr Greg Fox.

[24] George Johnson, 'Calvinism and Preaching' in *Evangelical Quarterly*, vol. 4, no.3, 15 July 1932, p. 249.

[25] W. Robert Godfrey, *John Calvin: Pilgrim and Pastor* (Wheaton: Crossway Books, 2009), p. 62.

[26] T. H. L. Parker, *Calvin's Preaching*, p. 62; Steven J. Lawson, *The*

William B. Evans and Dawn DeVries seem to exaggerate, albeit only slightly, when they say that the sermons, in Dawn DeVries's words, 'typically lasted for more than an hour'.[27] Calvin himself comments: 'I am naturally fond of brevity',[28] and on this point he criticised Martin Bucer (whom he much admired): 'He does not know how to stop writing.'[29]

Calvin's introductions in particular were crisp and to the point. Picking up on what had gone before he concentrated on the text at hand. And like any preacher, he would lament, as he did when preaching on 'Blessed are the peacemakers': 'Time, unfortunately, does not allow a more thorough treatment of this theme.'[30] In a lecture on Ezekiel 18:18-23, he abruptly

Expository Genius of John Calvin (Orlando: Reformation Trust, 2007), p. 120.

[27] John Calvin, *Sermons on the Acts of the Apostles, Chapters 1-7*, tr. by Rob Roy McGregor, introduction by William B. Evans (Edinburgh: Banner of Truth, 2008), p. xxi; Dawn DeVries, 'Calvin's Preaching', p. 106.

[28] Cited in J. Graham Miller (ed), *Calvin's Wisdom* (Edinburgh: Banner of Truth, 1992), p. 257, from *Institutes,* III,vi,1.

[29] Calvin, *Commentary*, Romans, 'Dedication to Simon Grynaeus'.

[30] John Calvin, *Sermons on the Beatitudes,* tr. by Robert White (Edinburgh: Banner of Truth, 2006), p. 61. So too John Calvin, *Songs of the Nativity: Selected Sermons on Luke 1 & 2,* tr. by Robert White (Edinburgh: Banner of Truth, 2008), p. 76.

concluded thus: 'The remainder tomorrow.'[31] At the end of his seventh lecture on Ezekiel, having reached Ezekiel 2:10, he suddenly stopped, saying: 'I cannot now proceed further, although what follows is connected with this subject.'[32]

There is a certain lack of structure in Calvin's sermons. Dawn DeVries writes of 'the somewhat haphazard organization that is customary of all his sermons.'[33] Andrew Blackwood suggests that the sermons might have been abler had he not preached so many.[34] Not for nothing does William Bouwsma describe Calvin as 'a driven man', an over-achiever who was almost overwhelmed with work.[35] Furthermore, <u>he was of a naturally retiring disposition</u>—although Herman Selderhuis perhaps exaggerates in saying he was not 'the giant of Noyon' but 'more like Tom Thumb'[36]—and only really lost his shyness in the

[31] Calvin, *Commentary,* Ezekiel 18:23; see too for Ezekiel 1:28 and 2:4-5.

[32] Calvin, *Commentary,* Ezekiel 2:10.

[33] Dawn DeVries, 'Calvin's Preaching', p. 116.

[34] Andrew Blackwood, 'Introduction' to Leroy Nixon, *John Calvin, Expository Preacher* (Michigan: Eerdmans, 1950), p. 6.

[35] William J. Bouwsma, *John Calvin: A Sixteenth Century Portrait* (Oxford: Oxford University Press, 1989), p. 29.

[36] Herman J. Selderhuis, *Calvin's Theology of the Psalms* (Michigan: Baker, 2007), p. 28.

pulpit. For all that, T. H. L. Parker waxes eloquent here:

> The sermons are like rivers, moving strongly in one direction, alive with eddies and cross-currents, now thundering in cataracts, now a calm mirror of the banks and the sky; but never still, never stagnant.[37]

Randall Zachman begs to differ, and sees a common structure of exposition, retention, and application.[38]

The evidence goes both ways to some extent, yet there is a general pattern to Calvin's preaching, which can be traced to what he detected in the prophets. In Hosea 4:1-2, the prophet brings charges against the people of God for trampling on his commandments. Israel, like all of us, required a mixture of promises of mercy and fulminations against sin. Calvin commented:

> We hence see that men cannot be taught, except God reproves their sins by his Word; and then, lest they despond, gives them a hope of mercy; and except he again returns to reproofs and threatenings.

---

[37] T. H. L. Parker, *Calvin's Preaching*, p. 132.

[38] Randall C. Zachman, 'Expounding Scripture and Applying It to Our Use: Calvin's Sermons on Ephesians' in *John Calvin as Teacher, Pastor, and Theologian* (Michigan: Baker, 2006), p. 149.

This is the mode of address which we find in all the Prophets.[39]

It is not the Lord who is changeable, but we who require frequent awakenings.

Calvin would tend to do a running commentary on three or four verses, although of the sixteen sermons included in Benjamin Farley's edition of Calvin's sermons on the Ten Commandments, from Deuteronomy 5, eight have only one verse as their text.[40] Narrative portions of Scripture supplied a larger number of verses upon which the sermon was based. In his 43 sermons on 2 Samuel 1-13, he only once preached on a single verse (2 *Sam.* 12:13); in this series his sermons usually covered 7-8 verses, although the very first sermon covered sixteen verses (2 *Sam.*1:1-16).[41]

It cannot be said that each sermon was always self-contained, with one central theme. The demarcation of some sermons seems a little strange. For

[39] Calvin, *Commentaries on the Twelve Minor Prophets,* vol. 1, Hosea, p. 137.

[40] See John Calvin, *Sermons on the Ten Commandments,* ed. and tr. by B. W. Farley (Michigan: Baker), 1980.

[41] Cf. John Calvin, *Sermons on 2 Samuel 1-13,* tr. by Douglas Kelly (Edinburgh: Banner of Truth), 1992.

example, in his sermons on Ephesians, he preached on Ephesians 3:20-4:2, then on 4:1-5, when the more natural break appears to be at 4:1, and 4:4-6 constitute a self-contained trinitarian unit.[42] Later, he preached on 4:23-26; a more natural arrangement would have been 4:22-24 (putting off the old man and putting on the new) and 4:26-27 (the subject of anger).[43] The first four pages of his sermon on 6:10-12 actually deal with the section on masters and slaves, from 6:5-9.[44]

In dealing with the hypocrisy of Ananias and Sapphira in Acts 5:1-11, Calvin preached one sermon on Acts 5:1-6, and the next on Acts 5:7-15. This latter sermon thus deals with the judgment on Sapphira (which takes up most of the sermon) and the miracles that the Lord performed through the apostles (which is dealt with in a somewhat rushed way at the end of the sermon).[45] In preaching on the role of women in the church, Calvin separates 1 Timothy 2:11 from 1 Timothy 2:12, which is somewhat disconcerting.[46]

[42] John Calvin, *Sermons on Ephesians*, pp. 303-32.

[43] John Calvin, *Sermons on Ephesians*, pp. 433-46.

[44] John Calvin, *Sermons on Ephesians*, pp. 648-52.

[45] Calvin, *Sermons on the Acts*, pp. 189-217.

[46] Calvin, *Sermons on the Epistles to Timothy and Titus* (Edinburgh:

He also deals with 1 Timothy 5:16-18 when verse 16 belongs to the previous section on widows, not with verses 17-18 on elders.[47]

Calvin's second lecture on the book of Jeremiah, dealing with Jeremiah 1:8-12, finishes in mid-air: 'It then follows,—but as the clock strikes, I cannot proceed farther today.'[48] Half of Ezekiel 16:50 is dealt with in lecture 47 on Ezekiel and half in lecture 48, with a curt comment at the end of the forty-seventh chapter: 'We must put off the remainder.'[49] At the end of his fifth lecture on Hosea, he suddenly says: 'But I cannot finish today.'[50] At the beginning of his eleventh lecture on Hosea, he commented: 'One thing escaped me in yesterday's lecture, on which I shall now briefly touch.'[51] He went on to discuss whether there were any legitimate priests in Israel because, in the division of the kingdom after Solomon's reign, the ten northern tribes had rejected the temple in

---

Banner of Truth (1579), repr. 1983), p. 211.

[47] Calvin, *Sermons on the Epistles to Timothy and Titus*, p. 211.

[48] Calvin, *Commentary*, Jeremiah 1:11-12.

[49] Calvin, *Commentary*, Ezekiel 16:50.

[50] Calvin, *Commentaries on the Twelve Minor Prophets*, vol. 1, Hosea, translated by Rev. John Owen (Michigan: Baker, reprinted 1979), p. 96.

[51] Calvin, *Commentaries on the Twelve Minor Prophets*, p. 157.

Jerusalem, where God was rightly worshipped. It reads rather like Calvin, after the lecture, recalled something that he should have said during the lecture—not an uncommon experience for preachers and teachers.

In dealing with Nathan's confrontation of David for his adultery and murder in 2 Samuel 12:1-6, Calvin preached quite incisively that

> it is not enough for God to use severity merely in order to convince us. For there are so many hidden things in us, there are twisted thoughts, there are haughty affections, and God must uncover all of that.

However, he breaks off quite suddenly: 'But these things cannot be discussed at present in detail. We will reserve them for another time.'[52] He then launched into the prayer after the sermon! It was hardly a compelling conclusion to the passage.

Calvin was aware of the problem, and as he began his series on Psalm 119, he resolved:

> For my own part, because I will frame myself to that manner and order which the Holy Spirit has here set down, I shall enforce myself to follow as briefly as I

---

[52] Calvin, *Sermons on 2 Samuel 1-13*, p. 533.

can the plain and true meaning of the text: and without continuing in long exhortations.[53]

Psalm 119, of course, consists of 22 stanzas, each consisting of 8 verses, and each beginning with a successive letter of the 22 in the Hebrew alphabet. 'Hence', declared Calvin, 'I determine by the grace of God to finish eight verses apart in every sermon.'[54]

We look in vain for the expected three headings, with various sub-headings. To indulge in an anachronism, Calvin was not a preacher in the Puritan mould. Theodore Beza recorded that Calvin possessed an extraordinary memory, and he seems to have relied on this in his preaching.[55] In 1559 John Crispin recorded that in Calvin's lectures (not his sermons),

> he occupied a whole hour in speaking, and was not wont to write in his book a single word to assist his memory.[56]

---

[53] Calvin, *Sermons on Psalm 119* (Audubon: Old Paths Publications [1580], repr. 1996), pp. 4-5.

[54] Calvin, *Sermons on Psalm 119,* p. 5.

[55] Theodore Beza, 'The Life of John Calvin' (*The Banner of Truth,* Issue 227-228, August-September 1982, p. 12).

[56] Calvin, *Commentaries on the Twelve Minor Prophets,* p. xxx.

Hence there is something inimitable about Calvin's preaching method, and not all of what he did ought to be commended to lesser preachers today.

Calvin's style was earnest, simple and lucid—Harold Dekker calls it 'delightfully plain'.[57] T.H.L. Parker refers to his 'familiar, homely style of preaching'[58]—not unlike that of Hugh Latimer. In his sermons on Deuteronomy, Calvin tenderly affirmed:

> We have the Scripture preached to us, and by that means God allures us sweetly to him, that he could not do any more for us, except he should take us onto his lap. We feel that he takes account of our weakness, chews our food for us, and speaks to us like a nurse.[59]

The preacher was, in a sense at least, to imitate God. To that end, Calvin was fond of idiomatic expressions. For example, he said of those who spoke against God:

---

[57] Calvin, *Sermons from Job,* p. xxiii.

[58] Parker, *Calvin's Preaching,* p. 140.

[59] Calvin, *Sermons on Deuteronomy,* p.146, as cited by Peter Adam, '"Preaching of a Lively Kind"—Calvin's Engaged Expository Preaching' in Mark Thompson (ed.), *Engaging with Calvin* (Nottingham: IVP, 2009), p. 16.

Is it not a perverting of the whole order of nature? Is it in our power to pluck the sun out of the sky, or to take the moon between our teeth, as they say?[60]

The sermons were meant to be understood by all and sundry. He did not aim to be a rhetorician, but a proclaimer of the unadorned truth of God.

Certainly, Calvin often preached with inadequate preparation. Hence he would make the occasional blunder. In the list of the works of the flesh in Galatians 5:19-21 he says that Paul moves from the grosser sins to the lesser ones. But Calvin's text included 'murders' in verse 21![61] In Acts, he preached on the need for generosity, and asserted:

If a man has a fountain in his house and can draw as much as he needs from it, he will be an ungrateful man unless he lets it flow out so his neighbours can share in it.

However, the text he cites is Proverbs 5:15-17, which refers to sexual relations within marriage.[62] In preaching on Ephesians 6:5-9 he gave a cross reference to 1 Corinthians 5 when he presumably meant 1

[60] Calvin, *Sermons on Ephesians*, p. 25.
[61] Calvin, *Sermons on Galatians*, p. 541.
[62] Calvin, *Sermons on the Acts*, p. 78.

Corinthians 6.[63] In 2 Samuel 6:6-12, he stated that 'The very angels of paradise are confused in looking at the glory God, and have their faces hidden, according to the description of the prophet Ezekiel.'[64] Actually, the reference is closer to Isaiah 6:2 than to Ezekiel 1. Sometimes, like any preacher, he is simply guilty of making a slip of the tongue. In preaching on Genesis, he stated: 'As our Lord Jesus Christ points out, children were always circumcised on the eighth day.'[65] Presumably, he was referring to the Old Testament, and to Leviticus 12:3. While preaching on Luke 2:9-14, he said: 'As we read in John, "He did not spare his only Son, but delivered him up to death for us."'[66] The reference is actually closer to what Paul says in Romans 8:32 than it is to anything in John's writings. Indeed, even in his letter to King Edward VI of England, which accompanied his exposition of Psalm 87, Calvin inadvertently referred to it as Psalm 78![67]

[63] Calvin, *Sermons on Ephesians,* p. 641.

[64] Calvin, *Sermons on 2 Samuel 1-13,* p. 246.

[65] Calvin, *Sermons on Genesis 1-11,* tr. by Rob Roy McGregor (Edinburgh: Banner of Truth, 2009), p. 132.

[66] Calvin, *Songs of the Nativity,* p. 144.

[67] Calvin, *Faith Unfeigned,* p. 109.

Nor was his exegesis always entirely convincing. Whatever views one takes of the use of musical instruments in public worship, Calvin's arguments are less than compelling. He wrote:

> To sing the praises of God upon the harp and psaltery unquestionably formed a part of the training of the law, and of the service of God under that dispensation of shadows and figures; but they are not now to be used in public thanksgiving. We are not, indeed, forbidden to use, in private, musical instruments, but they are banished out of the churches by the plain command of the Holy Spirit, when Paul, in 1 Cor. xiv. 13, lays it down as an invariable rule, that we must praise God, and pray to him only in a known tongue.[68]

He put musical instruments in the same class as sacrifices, candelabra, lamps, and similar things: it was to be 'nothing but mimicry if we followed David today in singing with cymbals, flutes, tambourines and psalteries.' In his own vigorous way, he denounced this as being 'apes without discretion'.[69]

---

[68] Calvin, *Commentary,* Psalm 71:22.
[69] Calvin, *Sermons on 2 Samuel 1-13*, pp. 241-42.

Systematic Expositor of Scripture

To cite Calvin: 'Our faith must be totally grounded upon that Word, as much as it would be if the heavens had opened a hundred thousand times and revealed the glory of God.'[70] Characteristically, he preached on his first Sunday in September 1541 from the text he had reached in his series when he had been banished three years previously. Something similar occurred after Calvin fell very ill in October 1558, and could not return to the pulpit until Monday 12 June 1559. Predictably, he did so continuing the exposition of Isaiah that he had been forced to leave off some eight months earlier. He rarely interrupted his series, except for Christmas, Easter, and Whitsunday, although with the minimum deviation.

Sixteenth-century Reformed Christians habitually spoke of 'going to sermon', and to Calvin, preaching was a solemn exercise of worship. As he put it in his series on the Acts:

The sermon is not a lot of hot air! One day we will have to give an account of all that we have heard

[70] Calvin, *Sermons on Galatians,* p. 16.

during preaching even though we have let it go in one ear and out the other.[71]

The solemnity of preaching needed to be felt both by the preacher and his hearers.

In preaching God met with his people, if the Word was truly preached. Indeed,

> When God's words be preached to us by men, let us receive it as if we saw his majesty face to face . . . we must not take the gospel as a doctrine bred here below, but we must always have God's majesty before our eyes.[72]

The preacher's calling is the highest possible calling: 'God speaks to us by the mouth of a man, and graciously shows himself here among us, and has a mortal man as his messenger.'[73]

The Authority of the Preacher

As we have seen, Calvin asserted that the power of the church is 'not infinite but subject to the Lord's

---

[71] Calvin, *Sermons on the Acts,* p. 182 (on *Acts* 4:32-37).

[72] Calvin, *Sermons on Deuteronomy,* p. 255, as cited in *Engaging with Calvin,* p. 22.

[73] Calvin, *Sermons on Timothy and Titus,* p. 269, as cited in *Engaging with Calvin,* p. 23.

Word and, as it were, enclosed within it'.[74] The differences between the apostles and their successors can be found in that

> the former were sure and genuine scribes of the Holy Spirit, and their writings are therefore to be considered oracles of God; but the sole office of others is to teach what is provided and sealed in the Holy Scriptures.[75]

Pastors, therefore, are to speak with both authority and humility:

> when a puny man risen from the dust speaks in God's name, at this point we best evidence our piety and obedience toward God if we show ourselves teachable toward his minister, although he excels us in nothing.[76]

> It does not matter if his word is ministered to us by mere mortals.[77]

Hence the divine authority of the church could only be located in the Word of God, not the preacher as such. Noting that God called Ezekiel to be faithful,

[74] *Institutes*, IV, viii, 4.
[75] *Institutes*, IV, viii, 9.
[76] *Institutes*, IV, iii, 1.
[77] Calvin, *Songs of the Nativity*, p. 70.

whether his hearers responded to him favourably or not, Calvin drew the lesson:

> We must learn, therefore, when God calls us to the office of teaching, not to regard the conduct of mankind. For if it please God to exercise us while we strive with the rebellious and refractory, yet God's word must be uttered, because he commands it.[78]

The preacher is called upon to be faithful to God before he is sensitive to the seeker. Preaching on Galatians, Calvin stated:

> Peace and friendship amongst men is a wonderful thing . . . At the same time, however, God's truth ought to be so precious to us that even if we had to set the whole world on fire in order to promote it, we should be only too willing to do so!'[79]

He added that 'the most important thing is that God's truth should be known.'[80]

> It were better that the preacher were mute and unable to speak and that the congregation heard nothing at all, than for them to listen to a man speak who has not been sent by God.[81]

[78] Calvin, *Commentary*, Ezekiel 2:7.
[79] Calvin, *Sermons on Galatians*, p. 117 (on *Gal.* 2:3-5).
[80] Calvin, *Sermons on Galatians*, p. 118 (on *Gal.* 2:3-5).
[81] Calvin, *Sermons on Galatians*, p. 411.

In commenting on 2 Corinthians 5:19-20, Calvin did not adopt the position that became Calvinistic orthodoxy, namely that the ambassadors are the apostles. Rather, Calvin asserted that

> the ministers of the church are ambassadors, for testifying and proclaiming the benefit of reconciliation, only on this condition—that they speak from the gospel, as from an authentic register.

Calvin saw a transmission of authority, that those who hear Christ's apostles hear the Messiah himself (*Luke* 10:16). However, he did not restrict the scope of the passage to apostles only but to pastors also.[82] There is, therefore, in Calvin's writings, a view of preaching which Peter Ward calls 'a kerygmatic real presence'.[83]

All revelation of God outside of Scripture is uncertain. Scripture alone is the sufficient Word of God:

> let us remember to observe one rule of modesty and sobriety, which is, not to speak, or think, or even desire to know, concerning obscure subjects,

[82] Calvin, *Commentary,* 2 Corinthians 5:19-20.
[83] Peter Ward, 'Coming to Sermon: The Practice of Doctrine in the Preaching of John Calvin', in *Scottish Journal of Theology,* vol. 58, no. 3, 2005, pp. 319, 332.

anything beyond the information given us in the divine Word.[84]

Hence, 'we ought to play the philosopher soberly and with great moderation'.[85] Those preachers who failed to nourish their people with God's Word are compared to a drunken and whoring nurse who loses her milk and fails to nourish her child.[86]

The Spiritual Walk of the Preacher

Calvin maintained that 'To be good theologians we must lead a holy life.'[87] Regarding pastors, he lamented: 'We may indeed choose a man and he shall perchance prove a beast.'[88] In preaching, therefore, Calvin would say that the message must apply to him first of all.[89] In his own lively and graphic way, he declared: 'It would be better for him to break his neck going up into the pulpit, if he does not take pains to be the first to follow God.'[90] On Galatians

[84] *Institutes*, I, xiv, 4.
[85] *Institutes*, I, xiii, 21.
[86] Calvin, *Sermons on Timothy and Titus,* p. 381 (on *1 Tim.* 4:6).
[87] T. H. L. Parker, *Calvin's Preaching,* p. 15.
[88] Calvin, *Sermons on Ephesians,* p. 370 (on *Eph.* 4:11-12).
[89] Calvin, *Sermons on Galatians,* p. 65.
[90] T. H. L. Parker, *John Calvin,* (Herts: Lion, 1977), p. 113.

1:10, he preached: 'This text exhorts all ministers of the Word to shut their eyes to the sinful desires of men if they wish to carry out their duty faithfully.'[91] In his view, 'ambition is the mother of all heresies.'[92] Hence he asked: 'After all, how could any of us make peace and calm troubles and disputes when they occur, unless we lead by example?'[93]

To Calvin, authority went hand-in-hand with humility and a good conscience. In his Epistle Dedicatory to John's Gospel, he wrote:

> Farther, as I freely acknowledge before the world that I am very far from possessing the careful diligence and the other virtues which the greatness and excellence of the office requires in a good pastor, and as I continually bewail before God the numerous sins which obstruct my progress, so I venture to declare that I am not without an honest and sincere desire to perform my duty.[94]

Calvin felt obliged to tell Cardinal Sadoleto that it was God who gave him the charge of the Church of

[91] Calvin, *Sermons on Galatians*, p. 60.
[92] Calvin, *Sermons on Ephesians*, p. 402.
[93] Calvin, *Sermons on the Beatitudes*, p. 53.
[94] Calvin, 'Epistle Dedicatory' in *Commentary on the Gospel of John*, tr. by William Pringle, vol.1, (Michigan: Baker, 1979), p. 19.

Geneva, and therefore he possessed what he called 'a legitimate vocation'.[95] All the necessary attributes of a preacher are found in Calvin—a sense of authority, a desire for godliness, love for God, and love for his people.

To Calvin, the preacher of grace must first be a man of grace. On Ephesians 4:31-32, he declared:

> For granted that another man has offended me, what then? Can I make myself out to be righteous and innocent, when I come before God? Alas, there are so many iniquities and transgressions in me that I should be confounded a hundred thousand times. Should one fault, then, committed against me, be unpardonable and shall a hundred, yes a whole million I have committed against God be nothing?[96]

It will be understood that Calvin was using 'I' and 'we' in a generic way to refer to all of us, but he was nevertheless still speaking first of himself.

In his sermons on Job, he explained himself most wonderfully:

---

[95] Calvin, and Jacopo Sadoleto, *A Reformation Debate,* edited by John C. Olin (Michigan: Baker, 1976), pp. 50-51.

[96] Calvin, *Sermons on Ephesians,* p. 484.

I am not here for myself alone. It is true that we should all profit in common, for when I mount to the pulpit it is not to teach others only. I do not withdraw myself apart, since I should be a student, and the Word that proceeds from my mouth should serve me as well as you, or it is the worse for me.[97]

Not Heavy-handed

In his sermons on Micah, preached late in the year 1550, Calvin warns against any minister who is swayed by self-gain: 'Like a muzzled dog, he will not cry out, though God is offended.'[98] Hence there was to be vigour and courage on the part of the preacher because 'the true role of the Word of God is to remonstrate with everyone (*sic*) for their sins.'[99] Vices were not to be ignored but denounced. Granted such a view, it should come as no surprise that Calvin's preaching was not for the faint-hearted. In August 1550, while preaching on Acts 6:1-3, he launched into a ferocious attack on those who mistreated the poor:

[97] Cited from the 95th sermon on Job by Bernard Cottret, *Calvin: A Biography*, p. 294.
[98] Calvin, *Sermons on the Book of Micah*, tr. and ed. by Benjamin Wirt Farley (Phillipsburg: P & R Publishing, 2003), p. 178.
[99] Calvin, *Sermons on Micah*, p. 169.

We see people who want to please men and play at being good servants, but who will hold back the goods dedicated to the poor and let them languish. Let the devil take such 'good managers' if they are not careful to do what they should! Let the devil take them!'[100]

William Naphy makes much of this side of Calvin's preaching, and emphasises the polemical nature of what he calls Calvin's 'verbal assaults'.[101]

In truth, Calvin knew that the task of a preacher was multi-faceted. In his commentary on Titus 1:9 he explained:

The pastor ought to have two voices: one, for gathering the sheep; and another, for warding off and driving away wolves and thieves. The Scripture supplies him with the means of doing both; for he who is deeply skilled in it will be able both to govern those who are teachable, and to refute the enemies of the truth.[102]

Preaching on the same text, he stated:

[100] Calvin, *Sermons on the Acts,* p. 308.
[101] William G. Naphy, *Calvin and the Consolidation of the Genevan Reformation* (Louisville: Westminster John Knox Press, 2003), pp. 153-62.
[102] Calvin, *Commentary,* Titus 1:9.

We must labour to instruct with all meekness them that are content to be governed by God, yes, and though they be weak we must bear with them; but if they come to be rebels, a sturdy horse must have a sturdy overseer.[103]

In Calvin's view of the ministry, there are times to be tender and times to be decided.

In dealing with those whom he called 'Nicodemites'—evangelical believers who still attended the Catholic Mass for reasons of safety—Calvin could be both blunt and compassionate. He declared: 'I must speak in even cruder terms to such blockheads. They hold that disguise is legitimate when one is among the papists.' On the same subject, he could write to a friend:

Yet I am not so excessively severe as to condemn all Christians who do not quit their country when subject to such bondage, as if I completely despaired of their salvation. I would, however, urge them at the very least to make a careful reckoning by honestly examining their consciences, and by truthfully

[103] John Calvin, *Sermons on Timothy and Titus* (Edinburgh: Banner of Truth, 1579, reprinted 1983), p. 1099 (spelling modernized). The English translation actually uses the word 'iade' or 'jade', which refers to an old or unruly horse.

recognizing how far they are from serving God as they should.

One ought not be beguiled into thinking that the Lord's Supper with its celebration of the once for all perfect sacrifice of Christ is anything like the Mass where, supposedly, Christ is repeatedly sacrificed. To Calvin, the Mass is 'like a harlot who passes herself off as a virtuous woman by sheltering under her husband's good name.'[104]

For all that, Calvin was not authoritarian in his exegesis. In 1539 he wrote to Simon Grynaeus in order to defend his decision to go ahead with the publication of his comparatively brief commentary on Romans:

> But since the variation of thought which we find in the human mind makes certain things more pleasing to some than to others, let each of my readers here use his own judgment, provided no one wants to force all others to obey his own rules.[105]

[104] Calvin, *Faith Unfeigned*, p. 16.

[105] Calvin, *The Epistle of Paul the Apostle to the Romans and Thessalonians,* tr. by Ross Mackenzie (Michigan/Carlisle: Eerdmans/Paternoster Press, 1995), p. 1.

Lest it be thought that he was embracing relativistic views, Calvin warned:

> If it be considered a sin to corrupt what has been dedicated to God, we assuredly cannot tolerate anyone who handles that most sacred of all things on earth with unclean or even ill-prepared hands.[106]

It was his practice not to press points which were unclear. In his sermons on First Timothy, Calvin declared:

> And when we come to hear a sermon, or take the holy Scriptures in hand to read them, that we should not be so foolish and proud, as to think we will perceive all that is told us, and all that we read, by our own fancy, but come to it reverently, waiting wholly upon God, knowing well that we have need to be taught by his Spirit, and without him, we can in no wise comprehend that which is taught us in his Word.[107]

From Galatians 1:6, Calvin saw 'no great significance' as to whether Paul meant the one who

---

[106] Calvin, *The Epistle of Paul the Apostle to the Romans and Thessalonians,* pp. 3-4.

[107] Calvin, *Sermons on Timothy and Titus,* p. 303 (spelling modernized).

called the Galatians was Christ or the Father.[108] He famously warned against pressing with too much curiosity into the subject of predestination.[109] Paul describes Christ as 'the end of the law' in Romans 10:4, and Calvin comments, quite mildly:

> The word completion, or perfection, as Erasmus has translated it, is, I think, quite appropriate in this passage. Since, however, the other reading has received almost universal approval, and is also quite suitable, I leave it to my readers to retain it.'[110]

The expression 'the righteousness of God' in Romans 1:17 and elsewhere has long been viewed as a crucial text, and has prompted much debate down through the ages, but Calvin did not write on it as though he wanted to alienate anybody who did not quite see it as he did. He wrote, again with great mildness: 'By the righteousness of God I understand that which is approved at his tribunal.' Then he added, no doubt with Martin Luther in mind:

> Some commentators explain the meaning to be 'what is given to us by God'. I certainly grant that the words

---

[108] Calvin, *Sermons on Galatians*, p. 38.
[109] *Institutes*, III, xxi, 2.
[110] Calvin, *Commentary*, Romans 10:4.

will bear this meaning, because God justifies us by his gospel, and thus saves us. And yet the former sense seems to me more suitable, although I would not spend much time on the question.[111]

Coming to Romans 10:14-17, he stated:

I shall not detain the reader long here in recounting and disproving the opinions of others. I shall state my own view freely, but each must form his own judgment.[112]

Regarding Paul's references to righteousness and holiness in Ephesians 4:24, he wrote clearly but without any overbearing spirit: 'I am rather inclined to make the distinction that holiness pertains to the first table of the law, and righteousness to the second.'[113] Regarding those who were appointed to stumble at the Word in 1 Peter 2:8, Calvin wrote of two 'equally suitable' views—that the Jews were

[111] Calvin, *Commentary,* Romans 1:17.

[112] Calvin, *Commentary,* Romans 10:14-17.

[113] Calvin, *Commentary,* Ephesians 4:24. Interestingly enough, in 1539, Calvin saw no such distinction at work in Romans 1:18 where Paul refers to 'ungodliness' and 'unrighteousness'. The two passages are not exactly parallel: Ephesians 4:24 is positive while Romans 1:18 is negative, and the word for 'ungodliness' in Romans 1:18 is not the negative of that translated as 'holiness' in Ephesians 4:24. For all that, it might be one of the few places where Calvin changed his mind in dealing with a biblical concept. See Calvin, *Commentary,* Romans 1:18.

appointed to believe but stumbled, or that they had been appointed to unbelief, as was Pharaoh in Moses's day.[114] When God says that he would make Israel like a desert (*Hos.* 2:3), it has been interpreted to mean either that Israel would be made as she was in the desert in the exodus, or she herself would be made like a desert. Calvin put forward both views, only adding that the latter was 'more approved'.[115] In his comments on Genesis 20:17, Calvin discussed the length of time that Abraham stayed in Gerar or Mamre, and then concluded: 'Yet, since the correct notation of time does little for the confirmation of our faith, I leave both opinions undecided.'[116] He never asserted any fanatical claim to possess insight into the clear and unambiguous meaning of every passage of Scripture. In dealing with the making of the tabernacle, he thought it puerile to philosophize on the mysteries of every hook and loop, for 'it is better to confess our ignorance than to indulge ourselves in frivolous conjectures.'[117] After Calvin's

[114] Calvin, *Commentary*, 1 Peter 2:8.

[115] Calvin, *Commentary*, Hosea 2:3.

[116] Calvin, *Commentary*, Genesis 20:17.

[117] Calvin, *Harmony of Exodus, Leviticus, Numbers and Deuteronomy*, vol. 2 (Michigan: Baker, 1979), on *Exod.* 26:1, p. 172.

death, Nicolas Colladon commented that the Genevan Reformer never preached on the Apocalypse because he did not understand everything in it, and added the same for the last chapters of Ezekiel.[118] In 1554 Calvin concluded a preaching series on Ezekiel somewhat uncharacteristically by covering the nine chapters of Ezekiel 40-48 in one sermon!

Turning to his *Harmony of the Gospels,* one finds Calvin often saying things such as:

It is not certain whether Moses represents Adam or God as speaking these words . . . [on *Matt.*19:5]

It is possible that he who is here mentioned had embraced the doctrine of Christ, and betaken himself to the performance of miracles with no bad intention [on *Mark* 9:38]

My opinion is this . . . [on the genealogies of Christ in *Matt.* 1:1-17 and *Luke* 3:23-38]

There are some, indeed, who give a different interpretation . . . For my own part, I have no objection to that opinion [on *Luke* 10:42]

If any one prefer to follow the opinion of those who conjecture that Christ repeated the same discourses

[118] Cited in E. A. de Boer, *John Calvin on the Visions of Ezekiel* (Leiden: Brill, 2004), p. 231.

on various occasions, I have no great objection [on *Luke* 11:53][119]

It should be pointed out that although Calvin employs such language more frequently in his commentaries than in his sermons, it does appear in both.

Calvin also expected other Christians to possess insights into Scripture. In his sermons on Genesis, he declared, from the prophecy in Joel 2:28, that

although we are like the scum of the earth . . . we also shall have the title of prophet, when we are true pupils of God.[120]

In a sense, every Christian is a prophet with a capacity for spiritual discernment and judgment. This helps to explain the involvement of laymen at the Friday morning Bible studies.

At times Calvin confesses himself to be at a loss over the meaning of some scripture. Christians must simply acknowledge their weakness and submit to God's incomprehensible counsel on such occasions. On Joshua 7:24, for example, Calvin acknowledged

[119] See Richard Burnett, 'John Calvin and the *Sensus Literalis*', in *Scottish Journal of Theology*, vol. 57, no. 1, 2004, p. 11.

[120] Max Engammare, 'Calvin: A Prophet without a Prophecy' in *Church History*, vol. 67, no. 4, 1998, p. 650.

that it seemed harsh, even barbarous and inhuman, that Achan's children perished with him. He also noted the wholesale slaughter that took place at Jericho, and commented:

> The infants and children who then perished by the sword we bewail as unworthily slain, as they had no apparent fault; but if we consider how much more deeply divine knowledge penetrates than human intellect can possibly do, we will rather acquiesce in his decree, than hurry ourselves to a precipice by giving way to presumption and extravagant pride.[121]

Sometimes all the preacher can do is bow before the unsearchable wisdom of the God who is both rich in mercy and righteous in judgment.

Calvin himself kept Sunday as the Lord's Day, but he was not harsh or legalistic on the issue: 'we ought to observe this order of having some day of the week, whether one or two. But all of that can be left up to the liberty of Christians.'[122] As it stands, that may be a little misleading as to Calvin's attitude to the Lord's Day, but it does reveal his refusal to dogmatise beyond what he thought the text was saying. Regarding

---

[121] Calvin, *Commentary*, Joshua 7:24.
[122] Calvin, *Sermons on the Ten Commandments*, p.111.

the strange providences of the book of Job, Calvin repeatedly cited 1 Corinthians 13:12 to describe the difficulty in reading providence in the midst of history.[123] Calvin possessed a sense of how nuanced and ambiguous life can be. Job's three friends, for example, teach good doctrine (the transcendence and righteousness of God, the sinfulness of man, the just order of history, and the reality of providence) yet they did so wrongly.[124]

The Reformer of Geneva was not afraid to adopt slightly unconventional views. In his Ecclesiastical Ordinances of 1541, Calvin viewed the deacon as one of the four offices of the church, the other three being doctor (or teacher), pastor, and elder. Indeed, Calvin saw two kinds of deacons—'one to serve the church in administering the affairs of the poor; the other, in caring for the poor themselves.'[125] The former was called a 'procurator' and the latter an 'hospitaller'.

[123] Susan E. Schreiner, '"Through a Mirror Dimly": Calvin's Sermons on Job' in *Calvin Theological Journal*, vol. 21, no. 2, November 1986, p. 179.

[124] See Susan Schreiner, 'Calvin as an interpreter of Job' in *Calvin and the Bible*, pp. 53-84.

[125] *Institutes*, IV, III, 9. The references to deacons in the 1541 Ordinances can be found in J. K. S. Reid (ed.), *Calvin: Theological Treatises* (Westminster Press, Philadelphia, repr. 1954, pp. 64-6).

Calvin tried to find justification for the two types of deacons in Romans 12:8, with the procurator contributing in liberality and the hospitaller performing acts of mercy with cheerfulness.[126] He considered that the widows of 1 Timothy 5 could serve the church as deacons in this second sense,[127] and in his sermons on 1 Timothy 5, he lamented that 'there was in those days that (which) we have not now.'[128]

Calvin understood 'the poor in spirit' in Matthew 5:3 not to mean those who have no confidence in themselves but those whose circumstances have been made poor by God. In Calvin's view, 'prosperity puffs us up with pride and ambition'. [129] In adopting this interpretation, Calvin departed, albeit not radically, from the views of Jerome, Chrysostom, Augustine, and Erasmus. Whereas many exegetes have understood Luke 6:20 ('Blessed are the poor') in terms of Matthew 5:3 ('Blessed are the poor in spirit'), Calvin understood it the other way round.

[126] Calvin, *Commentary*, Romans 12:8.
[127] *Institutes*, IV, III, 9.
[128] Calvin, *Sermons on Timothy and Titus*, p. 450. The quotation has been slightly modernized.
[129] Calvin, *Sermons on the Beatitudes*, pp. 20-21.

In T. H. L. Parker's summary:

> There is no threshing himself into a fever of impatience or frustration, no holier-than-thou rebuking of the people, no begging them in terms of hyperbole to give some physical sign that the message has been accepted. It is simply one man, conscious of his sins, aware how little progress he makes and how hard it is to be a doer of the Word, sympathetically passing on to his people (whom he knows to have the same sort of problems as himself) what God has said to them and to him . . . Yet he is never weak.'[130]

His application, for example, on 2 Samuel 12:13 is especially tender and compassionate:

> Furthermore, if on some occasion we seem to have been abandoned by God, let us be especially aware of his inestimable goodness, in that he has given us his hand to draw us out of the depths of the hell into which we have plunged (*Psa.* 40:2)[131]

In Calvin's view,

> We must so temper our sermons that they may profit the hearers, for unless there be some hope of pardon

[130] T. H. L. Parker, *Calvin's Preaching*, p. 119.
[131] Calvin, *Sermons on 2 Samuel 1-13*, p. 564.

left, the terror and fear of punishment hardens men's hearts with stubbornness.[132]

The Centrality of Christ

To Calvin, Christ is the centre and goal of all Scripture. For, indeed, 'there is no salvation whatsoever outside of Jesus Christ, for he is the beginning and the end of faith, and he is all in all.'[133] 'Indeed, every doctrine of the law, every command, every promise, always points to Christ.'[134] The Passover, to cite an obvious example, points to Christ as the true Passover.[135] Having said that, Calvin was careful not to claim too much, and it is perhaps surprising to read his opening comment on Genesis 3:15, the *Protevangelium:*

> I interpret this simply to mean that there should always be the hostile strife between the human and serpents, which is now apparent; for, by a secret feeling of nature, man abhors them.

[132] Calvin, *Commentary,* Acts 3:17.
[133] Calvin, *Sermons of Galatians,* p. 186 (on *Gal.* 2:14-16).
[134] Calvin, *Commentary,* Romans 10:4.
[135] John Currid, *Calvin and the Biblical Languages* (Fearn: Christian Focus Publications, 2006), p. 102.

He understood the seed of the woman in a collective sense rather than a specific prophecy of the Messiah.[136]

Furthermore, despite church tradition, he refused to link the kings from Tarshish and the isles bringing presents in Psalm 72:10 to the coming of the Magi from the east to the Christ child in Matthew 2:1-12.[137] Overall, it must be said that Calvin was restrained in his exegesis, never wanting to claim more than Scripture revealed.[138]

Calvin's faith was firmly centred on what God had revealed in Christ, but he did not strain Scripture to find the Messiah in a direct way in every place. In his sermons on Ephesians, he stated:

> So much the more therefore it behoves us to go to him, and when we read the holy Scripture, let the object we aim at always be to know what is the grace of God which he has shown us in the person of his only Son, and when we once know it, we shall have profited very well in God's school and may well cast away all other things as filth and poison.[139]

---

[136] Calvin, *Commentary,* Genesis 3:15.

[137] Calvin, *Commentary,* Psalm 72:10.

[138] See David Puckett, *John Calvin's Exegesis of the Old Testament* (Louisville: Westminster John Knox Press, 1995), pp. 1-24; and G. Sujin Pak, *The Judaizing Calvin* (Oxford: Oxford University Press, 2010).

[139] Calvin, *Sermons on Ephesians,* p. 299.

Calvin never lost his wonder at God's grace in Christ, and the ignominy to which Christ descended in order to save sinners. 'But these matters call for secret meditation', he said, 'rather than for the ornament of words.'[140]

Use of Vivid Imagery

Dawn DeVries seems wide of the mark when she writes of Calvin: 'His own preaching style, however, was usually grave, sedate, and unfocused—perhaps even ponderous.'[141] Herman Selderhuis's comment is a judicious response to this criticism: 'Calvin may be known as a fierce opponent of images in churches, but he was nevertheless a fervent proponent of images in preaching.'[142] Calvin complained about orators who concealed the truth, or who engaged in speculation, or who were overly subtle.[143] He aimed to speak with clarity and simplicity, and with a good deal of colour.

[140] Calvin, *Commentary*, Matthew 27:27.
[141] Dawn DeVries, 'Calvin's Preaching', in *The Cambridge Companion to John Calvin*, p. 121.
[142] Herman J. Selderhuis, *John Calvin: A Pilgrim's Life*, tr. by Albert Gootjes (Downers Grove: IVP, 2009), p. 114.
[143] Marvin Anderson, pp. 172-3.

With reference to the falling away of the Galatians, Calvin said that the devil seduces, like a rake with a young girl.[144] On Galatians 1:8-10, he declared: 'We may say that, even if the Pope and all his stinking clergy had the angels on their side, this would be nothing compared to the Lord Jesus Christ.'[145] Also, 'We do not need to go to school for vanity, for each one is a great professor on this subject.'[146] Writing of Calvin's *Institutes,* Quirinus Breen observes: 'Were one to name the most constant excellence of Calvin, it could well be that of vividness; he tries his utmost to keep the reader awake.'[147] The same can be said of his sermons.

In preaching on Galatians, Calvin declared that those who believe in free will think that God's grace is flying through the air like a tennis ball, and it is up to us to catch it.[148] In his commentary on First John, he remarked that until our minds are cleansed, the exhortation not to love the world 'would be like

[144] Calvin, *Sermons on Galatians,* p. 5.

[145] Calvin, *Sermons on Galatians,* p. 53.

[146] Cited in Marvin Anderson, p. 176.

[147] Quirinus Breen, 'John Calvin and the Rhetorical Tradition' in *Church History,* vol. 26, March 1957, p. 8.

[148] Calvin, *Sermons on Galatians,* p. 135 (on *Gal.* 2:6-10).

pouring water on a ball; you can gather, no, not a drop, because there is no empty place to retain water.'[149] In warning against tyrannical husbands, he said: 'These are hangmen who will thus make the lives of their wives a hell.'[150] In his sermons on Ephesians, he referred to rich men who might own five thousand slaves in one house, leading him to comment that, if one was not careful, 'that was the way to have one's throat cut five thousand times'.[151]

Harold Dekker conveniently lists many of Calvin's lively and forceful expressions: 'When the devil lights the fire he also pumps the bellows'; intemperate young people are 'like young chicks hatched only three days'; the proud 'admire their feathers like peacocks'; God is like a physician who finds that 'no gentler means will serve than the letting of blood'; and 'We hop like toads and imagine ourselves doing like runaway horses.'[152] 'What are all the temples of

---

[149] Calvin, *Commentary,* 1 John 2:15.
[150] Calvin, *Sermons on Ephesians,* p. 570.
[151] Calvin, *Sermons on Ephesians,* p. 634.
[152] Cited in John Calvin, *Sermons from Job, selected and translated by Leroy Nixon,* pp.xxvi-xxvii. Calvin was fond of the 'toad' imagery—he called the popish clergy 'foul toads' (*Sermons on Galatians,* p. 279).

the Papists but brothels of Satan?'[153] We human beings are 'but worms of the earth', 'carrion and worth nothing';[154] 'We are but vermin and rottenness'.[155] Calvin held to what today would be called 'intelligent design', and spoke simply yet graphically: 'And if we but looked at the end of our fingernail, what artistry we would find there!'[156]

In describing Christ as the one who led captivity captive and who fills all things (*Eph.* 4:8-10), Calvin is rather graphic: 'Christ holds them, as it were, with his foot upon their throat.'[157] In preaching on Galatians 2:20-21, he asked: 'Do we wish to come to him? Then let us come empty-handed, for whatever we bring to him will be like smoke in our hands.'[158] Noting the falling away from grace of the Galatians, Calvin says, rather vividly: 'Let us not be like the cow who, having produced much milk, then breaks the churn and spills its contents!'[159] Calvin says that when

[153] Calvin, *Sermons on Galatians,* pp. 449-50.
[154] Calvin, *Sermons on Ephesians,* p. 573.
[155] Calvin, *Sermons on Ephesians,* p. 616.
[156] Calvin, *Sermons on Genesis 1-11,* p. 9.
[157] Calvin, *Sermons on Ephesians,* p. 358.
[158] Calvin, *Sermons on Galatians,* p. 215.
[159] Calvin, *Sermons on Galatians,* p. 242 (on *Gal.* 3:3-6).

it is a matter of salvation, 'men must not come like peacocks displaying their fantails, standing gazing at their own feathers!'[160] 'Men cannot help getting up on their high horse, as the saying goes, so as to show off and add lustre to themselves.'[161] 'We are but mean, mangy dogs, whom the Lord must totally transform.'[162] He called on his people to think through what it means to be all created in the image of God:

> Now would it be tolerated for a worm of the earth to esteem itself so much and exalt itself so far as to cry down its maker? . . . For the greatest folk in the world cannot say that they are made of any other stuff than that of all Adam's children.[163]

Regarding the relationship between the law and the gospel, as set out in Galatians 3:21-25, Calvin tried to stave off possible misunderstandings by saying that it was not like being offered a house for a price, then being told we can have it for nothing.[164] He also speaks of 'the tendency to imagine that we are

[160] Calvin, *Sermons on Galatians*, p. 352.
[161] Calvin, *Songs of the Nativity*, p. 43.
[162] Calvin, *Songs of the Nativity*, p. 60.
[163] Calvin, *Sermons on Ephesians*, p. 479.
[164] Calvin, *Sermons on Galatians*, p. 326.

little angels when we see that others are worse than ourselves, or at least when we see that they are no better'. And he quotes a sixteenth-century proverb, that we are all coal-sacks that blacken one another.[165] He warned against trying to preach beyond what we can know, to look for five feet on one sheep, as it were.[166] From Galatians, he declared that law and grace are like fire and ice: 'we cannot be justified by both the law and the grace of God!'[167]

Calvin painted images with his words: 'We have an insatiable desire to master things which are no business of ours, and our curiosity flutters like birds in the air.'[168] He was fond of everyday sayings, and so, in referring to our failure to work whole-heartedly and sincerely, he commented: 'we shall always have this back-shop with us.' A back-shop was behind the main shop, and was where secret business was conducted.[169] The desire to make men self-governing would, said Calvin, make us 'like mice in the straw'.[170]

[165] Calvin, *Sermons on Galatians,* pp. 587-88.
[166] Calvin, *Sermons on Ephesians,* p. 607.
[167] Calvin, *Sermons on Galatians,* p. 268.
[168] Calvin, *Songs of the Nativity,* p. 112
[169] Calvin, *Sermons on Ephesians,* p. 639.
[170] Calvin, *Sermons on Ephesians,* pp. 339-640.

In dealing with our need to press on to maturity in Christ, as Paul tells us in Ephesians 4:11-14, Calvin used a simple and concrete illustration.

> If a man were to shoot with a long bow or cross-bow, or with a fire-arm, and have no target before him, but were to shoot haphazardly this way and that way, what shooting that would be![171]

In preaching on 'Blessed are the meek', he imagines a worldly objector saying that 'it is not possible to deny our human nature: we must hunt with the hounds, because to be a sheep is to risk becoming someone else's dinner.'[172] Regarding persecution, he declared: 'We are like birds on a branch surrounded by many dangers.'[173] When he denounced the insatiable greed of some professing Christians, he put it most memorably:

> They would like to deprive others, so far as possible, of air to breathe and lock the sun in a box, so to speak, so no one can enjoy it but themselves.[174]

---

[171] Calvin, *Sermons on Ephesians,* pp.380-81.
[172] Calvin, *Sermons on the Beatitudes,* p. 34.
[173] Calvin, *Sermons on the Acts,* p. 118 (on *Acts* 4:1-4).
[174] Calvin, *Sermons on the Acts,* p. 76 (on *Acts* 2:43-45).

Naturally, the idiom of one age passes, and that can lead to some difficulties in translating Calvin's sermons. In saying that 'it is not for a man to struggle against the stream', Calvin's French actually said that it was not for a man 'to break the eel across the knee-cap'.[175] In dealing with translations, it is the idioms and colloquial sayings that can provide the most trouble—as well as some bemusement. Occasionally, Calvin would overload the image as when he referred to the proud: 'Their heart is puffed up like a toad, they fancy they are prodigies, they spread their wings wide.'[176]

Finally, in a sermon delivered on 29 June 1550, Calvin spoke of reverencing God's majesty:

> Now it is true that when it is a matter of coming into the church, we must not come as pigs to a trough, but with a deep sense of awe and humility. We must humble ourselves before the exalted majesty of God and not approach him as a bosom-buddy companion, as the saying goes.[177]

[175] Calvin, *Sermons on Ephesians*, p. 695.
[176] Calvin, *Songs of the Nativity*, p. 44.
[177] Calvin, *Sermons on the Acts*, p. 227 (on *Acts* 5:13-16).

Calvin managed to combine a sense of majesty with a rather homely style. At his best, there was a wonderful and memorable balance to his oratory. On 1 Peter 4:16 ('If we must suffer as Christians, let us glorify God for the blessing he bestows'), Calvin proclaimed:

> We are miserable earthworms, creatures full of vanity and liars into the bargain. Yet God would have us defend his truth, which is an honour not given even to the angels in paradise.[178]

Insofar as human beings can do anything to achieve this, Calvin's bringing together of the images of earthworms and angels would have the effect of presenting God's truth both simply and memorably.

Rhetorical Techniques

Calvin often asked questions of his people. For example, regarding the unity of the church (*Eph.* 4:6-8), he asked: 'And how may that be brought about?'[179] In a sermon on the Passover from Deuteronomy 16:1-4, he asked a series of questions:

---

[178] Calvin, *Faith Unfeigned*, p. 36.
[179] Calvin, *Sermons on Ephesians*, p. 334.

> What does baptism or the Lord's Supper bring us?
> Do they make the death and passion of our Lord
> Jesus Christ of more value than it is of itself? What
> help do we find in the bread, or in the wine, or in
> the water, to that purpose?[180]

Referring to Calvin's commentary on Ephesians, Zachman mentions Calvin's use of periphrasis (circumlocution), amplification, epexergasia (a kind of parallelism), hyperbaton (deviation from normal word order), epinikion (victory ode), apposition (use of additional noun to modify meaning), metaphor, emphatikoteron (emphasis), and synecdoche (figure of speech in which a part is substituted for a whole or a whole for a part).[181] This approach to Calvin's expositions is somewhat too formal. Where this can be seen as accurate, it would be due to Calvin's drawing on his many hours of study rather than a self-conscious attempt to call on the formal rules of rhetoric. For example, preachers are somewhat prone to exaggerate, and Calvin was no exception. Hence he complained of the eligible

[180] Cited in John Currid, *Calvin and the Biblical Languages,* p. 95.
[181] Randall C. Zachman, *Calvin as Teacher, Pastor, and Theologian,* p. 151.

women of Geneva: 'when they are to marry, they never give attention to the things that God shows and teaches them by his Word.'[182] It ought to be interpreted as the *sermonic* never rather than the *historical* never.

Calvin almost never told anecdotes in the pulpit. In his lectures on the Psalms, he did relate what he called 'a memorable story' in explaining Psalm 115:16 ('The heavens, the heavens are Jehovah's, but the earth he has given to the children of men'). Calvin recalls:

> While we were supping in a certain inn, and speaking of the hope of the heavenly life, a profane despiser of God happening to be present, treated our discourse with derision, and now and then mockingly exclaimed, 'The heaven of heavens is the Lord's.' He was instantly seized with dreadful pain, and began to call out: 'O God! O God!' He himself was then mocked until finally his pain receded.[183]

On Psalm 141:3-4 (which begins 'Set a watch, O Jehovah, upon my mouth'), he recounted a story attributed to Eusebius concerning a monk who, on reflecting on this verse, fell into 'the silly fallacy of

[182] Calvin, *Sermons on Ephesians*, p. 570.
[183] Calvin, *Commentary*, Psalm 115:16.

imagining that he had shown himself the perfect scholar by observing silence for a whole term of seven years.'[184] Preaching on Hebrews 13:13, he told of a young man who had lived for a time in Geneva, but was arrested and condemned to death in Tournai. He was offered two options: recant and be beheaded or adhere to the Reformed faith and be burned alive. He replied: 'He who will give me grace to endure death for his name, will surely give me grace to bear the flames.'[185] These three examples are exceptional, for it was rare for Calvin to adopt the stance of a story-teller.

When preaching through Genesis, however, he did give a somewhat extended treatment concerning how one may draw lessons from the life of birds. For example,

> In the case of storks, they feed their fathers and mothers in their old age, and that condemns the ingratitude of those who do not take into account the fathers and mothers who begot them. In birds we have an open school to teach us that we are monsters and against

[184] Calvin, *Commentary,* Psalm 141:3-4.
[185] Calvin, *Faith Unfeigned,* p. 47.

nature if we do not acknowledge those through whom God brought us into the world.[186]

According to Zachman, Calvin's favourite device in his sermons is

the imagined interior monologue, used first to show the way we think when we forget what God teaches us in his school, and then to show what difference it makes to keep the doctrine of God in our inmost thoughts.[187]

So, when dealing with the issue of assurance, Calvin preached:

Now this kind of hope is not something our own brains or imagination can devise. It would be foolish and rash of us to think: 'God will be good to me, because that is what my head tells me!' No, what we need is God's word which alone gives assurance.[188]

For all his sophistication as a thinker, the Genevan Reformer had the ability to treat complex issues in a simple way.

---

[186] Calvin, *Sermons on Genesis 1-11*, p. 78.
[187] Randall C. Zachman, *Calvin as Teacher, Pastor, and Theologian*, p. 172.
[188] Calvin, *Songs of the Nativity*, p. 62.

Attacking the doctrine of merit, Calvin imagined papists, Turks (Muslims), Jews and heathen all striving to win God's favour by being worthy.

> Well, let them boast! Let them appear before God with their noses in the air! All their merits, virtues and excellence will turn out to be mere filth, and all their works of satisfaction, worthless rubbish.[189]

No one in the congregation would have been left struggling to understand what exactly the preacher meant. Instead of saying that 'we are too easily made afraid and unbelieving', Calvin said: 'It only takes a fly to pass before our eyes for us to panic, and to make us feel there is no God in heaven to help us.'[190]

In his sermons, Calvin almost never quoted other authors openly. He did refer to the original Hebrew or Greek texts on occasions but never cited them, and was a master of paraphrase.

He could resort to ridicule. One of his most memorable efforts of such is to be found in his *Institutes,* where he cites Pope Innocent III's Fourth Lateran Council of 1215 which enjoined 'every-

---

[189] Calvin, *Songs of the Nativity,* p. 116.
[190] Calvin, *Songs of the Nativity,* p. 124.

one of both sexes once a year to confess all their sins before their own priest.' Calvin chuckled: 'this precept refers only to hermaphrodites, but applies to no one who is either male or female!'[191]

Occasionally he would refer to current events, as in his sermons on Ephesians in which he once noted that, the day before the sermon, a man was punished for selling Catholic trinkets.[192] On 27 January 1555, with council elections only a month away, he was preaching on 1 Timothy 5:1-3. In his sermon he lamented the spiritual condition of some who were standing for office:

> they will be first at the general council, and their voices shall be loudest of all, although they never showed any token of Christianity in all their lives.[193]

Calvin was not one to tell jokes in the pulpit but his sermons were not devoid of a certain kind of humour. He disliked luxury and indecency, and in a sermon on Ephesians 5:3-5 he poked fun at those

[191] *Institutes*, III, iv, 7.
[192] Calvin, *Sermons on Ephesians*, pp. 341-2.
[193] Calvin, *Sermons on Timothy and Titus*, p. 454 (spelling modernized).

dedicated followers of fashion. They dressed in such a way as to make it

> very hard to discern whether they are men or women. They appear in new dresses and trinkets, so that every day some new disguise is seen. They are decked in peacock-tail fashion, so that a man cannot pass within three foot of them without feeling, as it were, a windmill sail swirling by him.[194]

Although Calvin was ridiculing the decadence of certain sixteenth-century Genevans, his words are not lost on our twenty-first-century 'fashionistas'.

Addressing His Congregation

Calvin worked with a deep awareness that God's Word spoke to him, and so he spoke to his people. In his sermons on 2 Timothy, he declared:

> Therefore when I expound the Holy Scripture I must always compass myself by it, that they who hear me, may receive profit from the doctrine which I put forth, and be edified to their salvation. If I have not this affection, and if I do not procure their edifying who hear me, I commit sacrilege, and profane the Word of God.[195]

[194] Calvin, *Sermons on Ephesians*, p. 497.
[195] Calvin, *Sermons on Timothy and Titus,* p. 937 (spelling modernized).

Calvin was not writing for academia, but was bringing the Word of God to ordinary men, women, and youngsters. It first had to feed his own soul.

Calvin's usual practice was to use the language of the first person plural, namely the pronouns 'we', 'our', and 'us'.

> We should approach God as miserable beggars, if we would be justified in the name of our Lord Jesus Christ.[196]

On Galatians 1:10, he preached:

> Let us, therefore, desire to be spoken to earnestly, shown our sins, and made ashamed of them by having our guilt uncovered, rather than seeking to hear what pleases us.[197]

On Galatians 1:24 he said: 'may we all learn to glorify God when we see his grace in another'.[198] On Galatians 3:15, he declared:

> All our desires are twisted, perverse and full of rebellion; our senses are defiled by sin, so that, from the top of our heads to the soles of our feet we are full of corruption.[199]

[196] Calvin, *Sermons on Galatians*, p. 37.
[197] Calvin, *Sermons on Galatians*, p. 61.
[198] Calvin, *Sermons on Galatians*, p. 102.
[199] Calvin, *Sermons on Galatians*, p. 302.

He included himself in any admonition to remain faithful under persecution:

> We must be steadfast in resisting everything they can throw up against us and not be like weathervanes gyrating in the wind. Our faith must be constant and invincible, sustained by the word of God, which is everlasting.[200]

As a preacher, Calvin quickly reached his hearers. Noting the opposition that Noah faced, Calvin declared:

> Let us now take a look at ourselves. If we have a hardship that lasts three days, we cannot take it any more. We think God is putting too much on us. If we had to walk with Noah for a single year, not one of us would accept the burden. Each of us would clamour to be exempted.[201]

It could almost be said that he was quicker to apply than to explain. For example, preaching on Luke 1:45-48, he soon told his people: 'Now although this passage is about the Virgin Mary, it is relevant to each and every one of us.' Mary is unique in that

---

[200] Calvin, *Sermons on the Acts,* p. 117 (on *Acts* 4:1-4).
[201] Calvin, *Sermons on Genesis,* p. 599.

she bears in her womb the one who is sent from her God and Saviour, but she is also like every Christian in that she is saved through faith in this same God and Saviour. 'Faith, as Scripture describes it, contemplates God's promises.'[202]

On Ephesians 4:26-27, Calvin, who tended to be short-tempered at times, preached:

> For we are so fretful in ourselves already that a small thing will make us impatient. And therefore the fault that another man commits against us, however little it may be, will always put us in a temper. And why? Because we spend too much of our leisure looking upon other men's faults, and in the meanwhile forget our own.[203]

Indeed,

> For if it happens that a fly buzzes across our face, we are quickly in a spiteful temper, insomuch that no more is needed to make us fall out with everybody who does anything which does not please us.[204]

He commented vividly on how often we fail despite being provided with the armour of God:

[202] *Songs of the Nativity,* p. 20.
[203] *Sermons on Ehesians,* p. 447.
[204] *Sermons on Ephesians,* p. 445.

And why? Because God not only promises to succour us by his power, and that in such measure that we prove victorious, but he also puts means into our hands and arms us; and yet we hang up our armour on a hook![205]

From 1556 to 1558 he is reported to have referred only three times to 'I' in his sermons to scold his flock.[206]

Handley Moule points out that, in nineteenth-century Cambridge, the great Charles Simeon was able to avoid 'that easy but fatal mistake of troubled pastors, the scolding accent'.[207] So too did Calvin. Wilhelmus Moehn[208] has used a computer analysis of the frequency of certain words in sermons 9-25 from Acts. (See diagram on next page.)

Calvin included himself in any scriptural admonitions against sin. Hence he preached from Ephesians 4:17-19 that

> although we are slow to know our vices and would rather conceal them, yet we must understand that

[205] *Sermons on Ephesians,* p. 657.
[206] Marvin Anderson, p. 176.
[207] H. C. G. Moule, *Charles Simeon* (London: IVF, repr. 1965), p. 46.
[208] Wilhelmus H. Th. Moehn, *God Calls Us to His Service: The Relation Between God and His Audience in Calvin's Sermons on Acts* (Geneva: ET, 2001), p. 14.

Sermon #	9	10	11	12	13	14	15	16	17	18	19	20	21	22	23	24	25
Dieu	81	74	104	46	81	42	64	93	72	83	114	87	87	85	59	54	67
Jesus	25	24	0	4	12	4	1	1	13	12	17	39	10	21	7	10	10
Christ	25	24	0	7	14	4	1	1	13	12	17	36	10	21	7	11	10
Jesus Christ	0	0	6	18	34	7	4	1	0	1	3	4	2	0	0	0	0
nous	173	172	183	152	242	201	203	188	249	219	218	233	249	229	164	185	146
vous	1	13	13	0	0	1	0	0	0	6	6	3	0	0	7	0	3

it is more for our profit to come to reason, and to examine thoroughly what is in us.[209]

A close reading of Calvin's sermons reveals how he managed to avoid adopting any superior stance to his hearers, yet still be penetrating in uncovering sin in his hearers' lives. He knew his own heart: 'There is none so evil that he does not have a clever way of concealing his shamefulness from men.'[210] Ephesians 5:11 speaks of the need to rebuke or expose the unfruitful deeds of darkness, and Calvin did not hold back:

> I ask you, whether such silence does not sufficiently show that we are not worthy to eat one morsel of bread, nor to be counted in the number of earthworms, lice, bugs, and all the vilest and filthiest things of the world? Therefore let us think well upon it, that we shall be found guilty of the despising of God's majesty . . . because we do not rebuke men's vices.[211]

Indeed, Calvin knew the temptations of the preacher: 'there is not one of us who is not at fault in fearing men more than God.'[212]

[209] Calvin, *Sermons on Ephesians*, p. 407.
[210] Calvin, *Sermons on Galatians*, p. 606.
[211] Calvin, *Sermons on Ephesians*, p. 525.
[212] Calvin, *Sermons on Ephesians*, p. 528.

Calvin was highly critical of Catholicism but he was not dominated by a negative spirit, and so was aware of the danger of merely being anti-Catholic:

> To say that men may lawfully eat flesh on a Friday, and to mock all the superstitions of popery, and to say that they are but empty and trivial—that they can do with ease. But . . . if a man asks them what it is to be regenerate, what patience is, what newness of life is, and what it is to be fashioned again after the image of God—there the majority of them will show that they never tasted the truth of the gospel.[213]

His approach was pastoral, and, for example, he noted Paul's 'happy medium' in dealing with people, being neither dependent upon them nor indifferent to them.[214]

Yet he was blunt in warning against men who storm at their wives, and wives who are pert with their husbands 'like cats and dogs biting at one another'.[215] An acute observer, he added: 'It is a common occurrence in every house, and curses will

---

[213] Calvin, *Sermons on Galatians,* p. 424.
[214] Calvin, *Sermons on Galatians,* p. 92.
[215] Calvin, *Sermons on Ephesians,* p. 573 (on *Eph.* 5:22-26).

fly and move around.'[216] He possessed the preacher's tendency to see all evils in the Bible present in a greater way in his own times, and so he declared that 'theft is more rife nowadays in the world than ever it was'.[217] Also, 'every man and woman plays the bawd. When I say everyone, I mean that most men and women nowadays wink at all manner of evil and disorder'[218] — a remark that may owe something to the breakdown of the marriage of his brother Antoine, whose wife proved to be both unfaithful and cunning. Antoine and his family lived in the same large house as Calvin, but Antoine's marriage looked shaky in 1548 and collapsed completely in 1557. It proved to be a particularly distressing event for Calvin. He even complained there was 'a hundred times more integrity' back in the first century when Paul declared the days to be evil (*Eph.* 5:16)![219]

---

[216] Calvin, *Sermons on Ephesians*, p. 612 (on *Eph.* 5:31-33). See S. Lawson, *The Expository Genius of John Calvin*, pp. 110-111, for Calvin's blunt confrontation of the licentious refugees who arrived in Geneva.

[217] Calvin, *Sermons on Ephesians*, p. 455 (on *Eph.* 4:28).

[218] Calvin, *Sermons on Ephesians*, p. 529.

[219] Calvin, *Sermons on Ephesians*, p. 537.

In a sermon on Micah 3:9-10 he declared that there was less debauchery under the papacy before the Reformation.[220] In 1550 he pointed out the indifference and hostility to the hearing of God's Word: 'They would prefer to hear a bit of gossip than to hear testimony of their salvation.'[221] Once, during the afternoon sermon, he had occasion to admonish three 'hearers': 'Those three drunkards back there might just as well have stayed in the tavern, for all the good they are getting from listening to the Word of God.'[222] Calvin well realised the need to apply the Word of God to his hearers: 'Many people would like for me to preach with my eyes closed, not considering where I live, or in what locale, or in what time.'[223] However, he was thankful that the slavery of the Roman Empire was gone: 'we have great cause to praise God for taking away such bondage from among men.'[224]

---

[220] Calvin, *Sermons on Micah,* p. 172.

[221] Calvin, *Sermons on the Acts,* p. 97 (on *Acts* 3:17-19).

[222] Cited in Leroy Nixon, *John Calvin, Expository Preacher* (Michigan: Eerdmans, 1950), p. 65.

[223] Calvin, *Sermons on the Acts,* p. 327 (on *Acts* 6:1-6).

[224] Calvin, *Sermons on Ephesians,* p. 633.

In a sermon on Micah 2:6-7, we find Calvin's willingness to apply the Word with vigour and simplicity. He warned against those who professed the name of Christ but little else. He declared:

> Now this vice reigns today far more than it ever did in Micah's time . . . But the moment one stirs a stick in their dung, or uncovers their mischief, they despise such a person . . . Thus we witness today such untold murmuring against God and God's Word.[225]

Preaching had to be true and practical, and so he warned about being enamoured of old wives' tales and all curiosities 'which are good for nothing but to make men chatter as a pie in a cage'.[226]

On Job 38:1-4 Calvin declared:

> So then, to correct this arrogance that is in us, let us learn not to presume to answer our God; knowing that when we shall come before him, he will have the authority to examine us; indeed, according to his will, and not according to our appetite for it; and at our station; and that when he will have closed our mouth, and he will have commenced to speak,

---

[225] Calvin, *Sermons on Micah*, p. 101.

[226] Calvin, *Sermons on Timothy and Titus*, p. 383 (on *1 Tim.* 4:6-7; a 'pie' refers to a magpie).

we shall be more than confounded; let us learn to humble ourselves, so that we may be taught by him; and when we shall have been taught, may he make us contemplate his brightness in the midst of the shadows of the world.[227]

In Susan Schreiner's beautifully expressed summary of Calvin's sermons on Job, with their emphasis on God's strange providence:

> For Calvin, that trust had to suffice. By making Job the personification of human history, he extends Job's situation to that of his congregation. Standing within a history they did not understand, they could only confess a justice they did not see, and contemplate, as through a mirror dimly, a providence they would one day see face to face.[228]

Conclusion

William J. Bouwsma has written aptly of Calvin's 'talent for discerning analogies between other times and his own'.[229] He moved easily and quickly from

[227] Calvin, *Sermons from Job* (Nixon), p. 300.
[228] Susan E. Schreiner, '"Through a Mirror Dimly": Calvin's Sermons on Job' in *Calvin Theological Journal,* vol. 21, no. 2, November 1986, p. 193.
[229] William J. Bouwsma, *John Calvin: A Sixteenth Century Portrait*

the historical context to present application. This thread especially runs through his treatment of the Psalms. The struggles of the Psalmist quickly become the struggles of the Christian in Geneva. This same pattern can be found in his expositions on the prophets. To cite one example among many, in dealing with the false prophets in Ezekiel 13, he stated: 'What we suffer the ancients have experienced.'[230] Calvin never became bogged down in historical analysis for its own sake. Without losing track of the historical foundation, his preaching was always very contemporary. The Old Testament records that King Jeroboam I split off the ten northern tribes from the two southern tribes. To discourage his people from attending the temple in Jerusalem, he set up calves for worship in Dan and Bethel (*1 Kings* 12:28-30). Calvin soon drew a parallel with his own day: 'Christ's Supper and the papal Mass are as incompatible as Moses's sacrifices were with those of Jeroboam.'[231] Such an approach made his preaching vivid and relevant. Theodore Beza enthused in 1565, the year after Calvin's death:

(Oxford: Oxford University Press, 1989), p. 91.

[230] Calvin, *Commentary*, Ezekiel 13:1-3.

[231] Calvin, *Faith Unfeigned*, p. 13.

Who was shorter in teaching, and yet more solid—
more happy in solving difficulties, more vehement in
reproving, sweeter in consoling, and more correct in
confuting errors?[232]

Yet there is something greater than this. In all
Calvin's preaching, his ringing declaration was: 'Jesus
Christ is not half a saviour, he is the Saviour!'[233]
Calvin preached the gospel most warmly, and echoing
Paul's words in the final section of Galatians, he
pleaded:

> May we open our eyes to see our depravity and be
> ashamed of it, and not only so, but also to recognise
> that this life is nothing, and that God has placed us
> here as on a journey, so that he can test whether or
> not we are following him. May each of us therefore
> come aside, both morning and evening, to consider
> our sins, and may they be like goads to prick us and
> encourage us to come to God. May we not be like
> brute beasts, tied to this world, but may our need lead
> us to come to the Lord Jesus Christ. This is what it is
> to glory in the cross of the Lord Jesus Christ.[234]

[232] Calvin, *Commentary,* Ezekiel 13:1-3.
[233] Calvin, *Sermons on Galatians,* p. 451.
[234] Calvin, *Sermons on Galatians,* p. 649.

Calvin's motto was 'My heart I give you, promptly and sincerely.' To give one's heart to God, one had to submit one's intellect to God's revelation of himself in Scripture. This, Calvin sought to do. Then he sought to make known this revelation as a sinful, fallible human being proclaiming God's holy and inerrant truth. In a simple, lucid, direct, warm-hearted, and at times surprisingly unstructured way, Calvin proclaimed the glory of God and the freeness of his grace in Christ Jesus.

Appendix 1

Calvin's Love for the Word of God

I have hid your promise within my heart,
that I might not sin against you.
Psalm 119:11

When David speaks after this manner, I have hid your word or promise in my heart, he well declares that if we have but only a wandering knowledge, that the same will not hold us in, but that the Devil has by and by won upon us to oppress us, with temptations, and in the end to cast us down headlong. What must we then do? It is not enough that we have been at church, and heard what has been said there unto us, and that every one of us has mumbled unto himself something or another, but the word of God must be settled in us and be hid in our heart, to wit, that it may there be residing and continually abiding; and to have received it with such an affection, as that it be as it were imprinted in us. If this be not so, sin will reign in us, for it has by nature its habitation with us, for all our senses are wicked and corrupt, all our wills and desires are enemies unto God, unless God's word be well hidden in our hearts.

* * * * *

And my delight shall be in your commandments,
which I have loved. My hands also will I lift up unto
your commandments, which I have loved, and my
study shall be in your statutes.

Psalm 119:47-48

Lo here the principal point which we have to note, that we must take pleasure in the commandments of God which we have loved, to wit, that we ought to learn to conceive such an affection and desire to follow the word of God, and to stick to it, as that we should be fully resolved to say: 'In every deed, this is the most sweet and amiable thing that possibly can be, to subject ourselves under the yoke of our God and to bear it, and therefore we must draw in it, and obey him. Have we done this?

* * * * *

O Lord, your word endures forever in heaven.
Psalm 119:89

We see how changeable men are. It is very true that when we talk of the shadow, we may say that it moves and changes every minute of an hour, so that it does not rest; but if we look well and thoroughly search out that which is in the mind of man, we shall see there a great deal more vanity and change than is to be seen in the very shadow. And that which is more, David says in another place, that if man were laid in one school, and vanity in another, that vanity which is nothing would greatly weigh man down. And we shall not need to stand long disputing about this: For every man by his own experience can testify what it is, and what it can do, albeit there were nothing written nor yet anything thereof contained in the Scripture. What rests there then for us to do? In truth, we must seek for our constancy elsewhere than in ourselves.

Now God gives us a very good means if we will take it, which is, to build and settle ourselves upon his word. And for this cause it is, that the prophet Isaiah says: 'That the word of God endures forever' (*Isa.* 40:8). He had spoken before of the frailty and fickleness of men, as that nothing could be more; and although it might seem that there was some strength in them it is yet incontinent, clean, parched, and dried up, that it vanishes away into less than nothing. But he concludes, and says: 'That the word of God abides forever'. So then, see the means, how that men, although they be transitory and have no constancy at all in them, shall notwithstanding have a perfect constancy, and sure estate: namely, when as they shall stay themselves upon the truth of God and his word. According to this, it is here said: 'Your word, O Lord, abides forever in heaven.'

Some expound this, as if it had been said, that because the heavens have continued long, they render a good testimony of the truth of God. But here David speaks of the heavens, because we see by them a more manifest sign of the majesty of God than we see here below on earth. And indeed in that we are rude and earthly, we had need to have God to guide us, and to lift up our minds when he would have us to think on him, to the end that we might forget the world, and all the corruptible things here beneath. See then the reason why David in this place makes the seat and house of the word of God in heaven, because we had need to look a great deal higher than into our own sense, when we would comprehend how God is true and faithful. When we would feel the certainty and assurance of his word, we must enter into a deeper consideration than our sense is able to bear, and not look so into the visible thing, or into that which we conceive on earth.

* * * * *

Lord, what love have I unto your law?
All the day long is my study in it.
Psalm 119:97

See wherefore David adds that he was continually exercised in the word of God, meaning thereby to show how greatly he has loved it, as he has indeed said. And now we see what the example is which is here set down before us, for David speaks not this for himself, but tells us what we ought to be, if we will have God to instruct us, and to have him to make us partakers of his truth, wherein consists our whole felicity and welfare, for if we wax cold, and make no account of the word of God, we are not worthy that he should give us the least taste thereof. And for this cause, we must not marvel much, though so small a number in this day have profited in the Scripture.

Although every man desires to be praised and esteemed amongst men as very able and sufficient, yet for all that, we see what ignorance is in the greater number. And therefore there is good reason that God should shut the gate upon us, so that we might not have so much as the least entrance into his word. And why so? For where is the love and desire that David here makes mention of? Now when we shall know such a vice to be within us, we ought by and by to seek to amend it, and plead to God to put this coldness from out of our hearts, and that it would please him to enflame us in such sort, as that we might learn to prefer his word before all our fleshly desires, that we be no more so much given to all these vain follies of the world, but that we may look unto the principal thing.

* * * * *

My eyes gush with rivers of water,
because men do not keep your law.
Psalm 119:136

See then, that the true children of God ought not only to be contented with their own walking rightly, and to be framed according to the law of God, but they ought also by all means possible to labour to bring the whole world to that pass with them, to the end that all the creatures of God might with one accord reverence and glorify his majesty.

* * * * *

Call to prayer at the end of Psalm 119:9-16.

And according to this holy doctrine, let us prostrate ourselves before the face of our good God, acknowledging our innumerable sins, by which we continually provoke his heavy wrath, and indignation against us. Let us beseech him that it would please him to make us to feel our sins and iniquities more than we have done before, to the end that we might seek for such remedies as he has ordained for us in exercising ourselves about the reading of his holy word, and the daily preaching thereof which he has granted unto us.

And furthermore let us not forget to stir each other up to call upon him, to the end that by his Holy Spirit he might put his helping hand even in our hearts, and not suffer the doctrine which we hear by the mouth of his preachers, to become unprofitable to us, but that it may have the full power and strength so that we may from day to day be confirmed therein, and more and more learn to forsake the world, and all that may withdraw us from the union and conjunction of our Lord and Master Jesus Christ, who is our Head. And that he will not only show unto us this favour and grace, but also unto all people and nations of the earth.

* * * * *

Appendix 2

Calvin's Preface to the Geneva Bible of 1546[1]

Calvin to the Reader

If I were to write a long preface, I would make two points. My first point would be to stress that holy Scripture is a treasure of outstanding worth and infinite profit. In truth it is the foremost and most precious gift which we have in this world, for it is the key which opens the kingdom of God to us and which allows us to enter, so that we know who is

[1] I am grateful to Robert White for the use of this translation of Calvin's original French Preface.

the God we ought to worship and the goal to which he calls us. It is the path which safely guides us and which stops us spending our whole lives in pointless wandering. It is the true standard by which we tell the good from the bad, and which teaches us how we may properly serve God instead of going where the whim takes us, chasing like everyone else after worthless delusions and sometimes even choosing as objects of devotion the very things which God condemns as wicked.

Scripture is the light which directs us, the lamp which illumines us amid the world's darkness, lest we stumble miserably like the blind at so many obstacles which surround us and, what is worse, falter at each step. It is the school of all wisdom, a wisdom surpassing all human understanding and which fills the angels themselves with wonder. It is the mirror in which we behold God's face that we may be transformed into his glory. It is the royal sceptre by which God rules us as his people, and the crook which he gives to us as a token that he would be our shepherd. It is the instrument of his covenant which he made with us, freely committing himself in his goodness to be bound to us by enduring ties. It is the proof of his goodwill which gives rest to our consciences in knowing where our salvation lies. It is the only food for our souls which feeds them for eternal life. In a word, it is the only thing which makes us different from the heathen and from unbelievers, in that we have a sure religion which is founded on God's infallible truth. All other people are persuaded by dubious opinions or else grow hard and stubborn in their wilful unbelief.

My second point would be to say how important it is to get the most out of Scripture. Two things are required by way of preparation. First, we must ourselves be well disposed and clear about what we should be aiming at. For no one will ever be able to be taught by God if he does not come promptly and resolutely to him so as to follow all that is commanded him; if he does not forsake his own understanding and reason in order to be wise and teachable; if he does not curb his own wishes in order to obey the Master's pleasure; if, indeed, he does not surrender to God's will, and seek it out in order to make it a pattern for his whole life, in thought, word, and deed;

if, finally, he does not throw off all earthly cares in order to ponder spiritual things. And because our natural inclination is to do otherwise, we should commend ourselves to God to be led by his Spirit, without whom we study in vain and waste our time. But when we have the gift of the Spirit from God there is no reason to fear, because we are under the hand of so skilled a guide. We can be sure that God does not refuse his Spirit to those who sincerely ask him. Let us learn, then, to prepare ourselves in the way described.

Then too, if we would benefit from Scripture we must be careful not to circle aimlessly about without ever reaching the point of true understanding. So let us beware of idle speculation or time-wasting debates, which merely serve as Paul says to provoke strife and disputes (1 *Tim.* 6:4-5), or which torment the mind or which, under the guise of subtlety, send it soaring skywards while removing any solid foundation. For Scripture is not given to us to satisfy our foolish curiosity or to serve our personal ambition. It is, says Paul, useful. In what way? It instructs us in sound doctrine and comforts us, encourages us, makes us perfect in every good work (2 *Tim.* 3:16-17). Let us therefore use it to that end. If we are asked how it may edify us overall, the answer is that it teaches us to put our entire trust in God and to walk in his fear. And because Jesus Christ is the end of the law and the prophets, and the substance of the gospel, it teaches us also to aim at nothing less than knowing him, since it is clear that merely to step an inch away from him is to lose one's way.

What now prevents me developing these points further is that not just a preface but a whole book would be required for a really adequate explanation. It is enough, then, to have touched briefly on these—in passing as it were, for which I am sorry—and to have shown readers what it is useful for them to know from the moment they open Scripture.

OTHER CALVIN TITLES
FROM THE TRUST

COMMENTARIES

Genesis 978 0 85151 093 4
cloth-bound 1088pp

Commentary on the Psalms (Abridged)
978 1 84871 031 3, cloth-bound 684pp

Jeremiah & Lamentations
978 0 85151 552 6, 5 vol. set, cloth-bound

Daniel
978 0 85151 092 7, cloth-bound 808pp

Hosea
978 0 85151 473 4, cloth-bound 544pp

Joel, Amos & Obadiah
978 0 85151 474 1, cloth-bound 520pp

Jonah, Michah & Nahum
978 0 85151 475 8, cloth-bound 544pp

Habakkuk, Zephaniah & Haggai
978 0 85151 477 2, cloth-bound 416pp

Zechariah & Malachi
978 0 85151 476 5, cloth-bound 720pp

SERMONS

Sermons on Genesis 1:1-11:4
978 1 84871 038 2, cloth-bound 888pp

Sermons on Second Samuel 1-13
978 0 85151 578 6, cloth-bound 696pp

Sermons on Job
978 0 85151 644 8, cloth-bound 784pp

Sermons on the Beatitudes
978 0 85151 934 0, cloth-bound 128pp

Songs of the Nativity (Luke 1&2)
978 1 84871 010 8, cloth-bound, 280pp

Sermons on Acts 1-7
978 0 85151 968 5, cloth-bound, 688pp

Sermons on Galatians
978 0 85151 699 8, cloth-bound 688pp

Sermons on Ephesians
978 0 85151 170 2, cloth-bound 728pp

Faith Unfeigned
978 1 84871 086 3, cloth-bound 208pp

TRACTS AND LETTERS

Tracts and Letters of John Calvin
7 Volume Set
978 0 85151 987 6
cloth-bound 3488pp

Long out of print the republication of Calvin's *Tracts and Letters* will delight all who have come to appreciate the writings of the sixteenth-century reformer of Geneva. Three volumes of *Tracts* comprise some of Calvin's most important writings. The four volumes of *Letters* range from 1528 to the year of the reformer's death in 1564. Although they are of great historical interest, their permanent significance lies in the reminder they provide of a great work of God, and the example they set of compassionate Christian care, and a deep concern for the advance of the gospel wherever it is proclaimed. Calvin's personal ambition undergirds each tract and letter: 'It is enough that I live and die for Christ who is to his followers a gain both in life and in death.'